The Gift of Blessing

The Gift of
Blessing

Kate Patterson

Muddy
Pearl

First published in 2018 by Muddy Pearl, Edinburgh, Scotland.

www.muddypearl.com

books@muddypearl.com

British Library Cataloguing in Publication Data

A catalogue record for this book is available from the British Library

ISBN 978-1-910012-49-9

Cover image © Shutterstock: Anna Hoychuk
Interior illustrations by Healey Blair

Typeset by www.revocreative.co.uk

Printed in Great Britain by Bell & Bain Ltd, Glasgow

DEDICATION

To all my wonderful family and friends who have brought us God's love in
tangible ways as we have grieved the loss of Trevor. We have been, and are
being, carried by the hugs, cakes, flowers, meals in and out, food parcels,
texts, calls, precious cards, gifts and above all your prayers.

And especially to Johnny, Connor and Ben –
you are an ongoing gift of blessing to me.

"The Lord bless you
and keep you;
The Lord make his face shine on you
and be gracious to you;
The Lord turn his face towards you
and give you peace."

Numbers 22 : 24-26

PREFACE

This book, *The Gift of Blessing* grew out of *The Promise of Blessing*, which was written in 2015. We heard that after reading straight through the *Promise* book, people had then started praying over it a page at a time, so it seemed a natural step to make it into a devotional book.

The Gift of Blessing was put together in a time of joy after celebrating 25 years of marriage, but just after I completed it, my husband, Trevor, unexpectedly died. I have been carried through the past months by the truth that God is ever present – in the desert, in the storm and especially beside a coffin. Though my eyes have sometimes been too full of tears to see the Father's face, I have found that he is close to the broken-hearted. I am so grateful for all the ways that he has shown his care for us.

In whatever state of life you find yourself as you open up *The Gift of Blessing*, whether it is joy or sorrow, my prayer is that you will meet the one who is unswerving in his desire to bless you and keep you, to make his face shine upon you and be gracious to you, to turn his face towards you and give you his peace.

God's gift of blessing is for you, a gift more precious than any other gift you will ever receive. It will never go out of fashion or need upgrading; it is a gift of transformation. The source of all blessing makes us like himself – a blessing to those around us.

"Lord make your face shine upon us that we may shine with you."

CONTENTS

THE PROMISE OF BLESSING

Would you be surprised to discover that there is a promise of blessing for you?

The shining blessing of Numbers 6 is a gift from God to all his people – and that includes you. There are many blessings recorded in the Old Testament but this is the only one which comes directly from God himself. He asked his priests to pray it over his people and they have done so for centuries. God loves to bless those who turn to him.

Blessing is God's idea – it's the first thing that he did when he made Adam and Eve and it's the last thing that Jesus did before he ascended into heaven. Just as any good father wants his children to thrive, God loves you and wants to bless you. As John Newton's hymn, *Amazing Grace*, so beautifully puts it,

The Lord has promised good to me,
His Word my hope secures;

Today, God wants to shine his loving face upon you to light up your life and he gives you the wonderful words of this blessing in Numbers 6 as a gift.

'The LORD bless you
and keep you;
the LORD make his face shine on you
and be gracious to you;
the LORD turn his face towards you
and give you peace.'

God is inviting you to dwell in his blessing. Don't rush. Take your time and pray it over and into your life and the lives of those around you.

The Lord

bless you

Trusting the blessing

If we don't trust that God wants to bless us, we will be like millionaires in rags. If we live life expecting nothing of God, our heads will be down and we will miss what he has for us.

God wants each of us to have a rock-like certainty that we never need to twist his arm when it comes to blessing. He wants to build in you and me the breathtaking confidence of King David, who could boldly declare,

Surely your goodness and love will follow me
all the days of my life,
PSALM 23:6

God is not a grumpy old man who measures out blessing in measly thimblefuls. From the start, the enemy of our souls has constantly broadcast the lie that God doesn't want the best for us, and it is only too easy to tune into that wavelength. Choose to listen to the truth that God will never withhold his love from you.

 "Thank you, my loving Father, for your unfailing love and your promise to bless me."

THE GIFT OF SHALOM

All shall be well and all shall be well and all manner of things shall be well.
JULIAN OF NORWICH

Many people envisage the blessed life as a holiday in the Bahamas, but the Bible has a richer definition: the ancient Hebrew word *shalom*, a rich word which means well-being, wholeness and health, peace and welcome, home-coming and belonging, truth and justice. It is about *being* not just *having*. It speaks of the deep contentment of a child who is well fed and wrapped up secure in their parent's arms.

King David understood that this deep contentment comes from childlike trust:

My heart is not proud, LORD,
my eyes are not haughty;
I do not concern myself with great matters
or things too wonderful for me.
But I have calmed and quietened myself,
… like a weaned child I am content.
PSALM 131:1—2

Read these verses aloud slowly and deliberately.
Entrust all the desires of your heart, the worries of your day
and your greatest hopes to the one who cares for you.

THE GIFT OF WELL-BEING

'The LORD be exalted,
who delights in the well-being of his servant.'
PSALM 35:27

God DELIGHTS in your well-being. It brings him joy to see you secure, peaceful, thriving and content. That's why he is always speaking blessing over our lives. *Consider the extraordinary truth that your well-being matters to God.* Why? Because he loves you even more than the very best dad loves his kids.

We can trust this truth even when life is tough. The writer of Psalm 35 was in the midst of difficulty yet still chose to trust that God cared about his well-being. So when it's hard, join John Piper and preach a sermon to your soul,

Soul, be glad today! Be strong! Look, do you see the greatness of the Lord God Almighty? Do you see the power of the Maker of heaven and earth? Do you see the wisdom and the knowledge of the one who designed the universe and the molecule? Well, hear this and be astounded, little soul: that great God delights in your welfare! Did you hear that, little soul? I said, 'Delights!' That's D-E-L-I-G-H-T-S, DELIGHTS! Your welfare is not his duty; it's his joy![1]

 "O my soul, trust that your Father delights in you."

THE GIFT OF INTIMACY

Come near to God
and he will come near to you.
JAMES 4:8

Intimacy is scary because it means 'into me see', yet we desire intimacy because it's what we were made for. When God first created Adam, the one thing that was 'not good' was for man to be alone. Adam celebrated Eve as bone of his bone, flesh of his flesh, no barriers, no hidden agendas, no secrets, no shame, no fear. That's intimacy.

We were created for intimacy with God, to know God and to be known by him, to love and to be loved.

Today, God invites us to live in unbroken communion with him, knowing that he is near all the time. He wants you to know the overwhelming joy of being constantly and deeply loved.

There is not in the world a kind of life more sweet and delightful
than that of a continual conversation with God.[2]

Our deepest contentment comes from intimacy with our Maker. If you will quieten your heart to his voice, God is calling you to himself.

 What do you want to tell the one who loves you best?

17

THE GIFT OF SIGNIFICANCE

Deep down we know we are destined for more than the dust. Buried deep within our hearts are desires so fierce that no godless universe could ever explain them. Mere survival of the fittest does not begin to satisfy because our blueprint is the imprint of God. We know we want significance; we want to make a difference. That's why God has appointed good works for us to do. The great Creator made us in his image to be fruitful just as he is – to bear lasting fruit (John 15:16).

The way to this fruitfulness is delightful. It comes not from striving but from entering into intimacy with our Maker.

 "Loving Saviour, may I remain in you today."

The gift of God's favour

Jesus began his ministry with words that shatter all our fears that God might not want to bless us. He came 'to proclaim the year of the Lord's favour' (Luke 4:19).

We can mistakenly think that God has favourites – 'good' people, people like Abraham, to whom he said, 'I will bless you'.

But God's blessing is never exclusive. God told Abraham that he would not only bless Abraham but make him a blessing to the whole world! Jesus was born as a descendant of Abraham and the promise was fulfilled.

God's favour always reaches out to draw others in. Blessing from God to us, blessing from God through us: that is the plan.

He redeemed us in order that the blessing given to Abraham might come to the Gentiles through Christ Jesus, so that by faith we might receive the promise of the Spirit.

GALATIANS 3:14

 "Father, I thank you that you never exclude me. I am included in your promise of blessing."

WORDS OF POWER

We know human words have power to savagely wound us or to build us up. How much more power has the word of God? Spoken by the one whose Word propelled the universe into motion, his words of blessing create and restore. Our God 'calls into being things that were not' (Romans 4:17).

God spoke our universe into existence: from emptiness came a universe that it would take more than 46 BILLION light years to cross! From nothingness came whirling galaxies, spiralling DNA and you and me! But even more wonderful for us is that God's voice can recreate us!

A flaky, foolhardy fisherman named Simon was recreated with a new name, Peter, which means 'the Rock', and founded the church. Nicodemus, the fearful Pharisee, was reborn and finally stood out as the disciple who had the courage to ask Pilate for Jesus' body. Saul, the Christian-killer was renamed by God as Paul, the apostle to the Gentiles. God's word has unlimited power to transform.

If God speaks over you that you are a new creation, you are made new. So which voices will you listen to? Voices that tear you down or God's voice of blessing telling you that you are his beloved child?

Let the morning bring me
word of your unfailing love,
for I have put my
trust in you.

Psalm 143:8

BLESSING PREVAILS

There is one big question that lingers – if God is so eager to bless us, why is there so much anguish in our world? The Bible begins by telling us that God made a perfect world, which he handed over to our care. When people rejected God's rule, it all went askew. Blessing was refused, design marred, intimacy wounded, significance squandered and fruitfulness made barren. Our intimacy with God was abandoned for self-satisfaction, our delegated authority was thrown aside for self-rule and we picked a poisoned fruit in place of eternal fruitfulness. Paradise was lost to us and our ultimate destination proves not to be a neutral no-man's land but exile into the enemy territory of the curse. That is why Jesus described Satan as 'the prince of this world' (John 14:30).

Yet God is so committed to his blessing-plan that he came in Christ to take the curse on himself. Blessing prevails.

With the goodness of God to desire our highest welfare, the wisdom of God to plan it, and the power of God to achieve it, what do we lack? Surely we are the most favoured of all creatures.

A W TOZER, *THE KNOWLEDGE OF THE HOLY*

"Father, when I consider how Christ was cursed that I might be blessed, I am overwhelmed by your love. I praise you that you gave all that we might have all."

God's invitation

God didn't force his blessing upon his creation. He wanted us free to choose him. When humanity refused him, he could have scrapped the world and started again, but he wanted a world with you in it. So he came himself in Christ with the most vulnerable request,

'Will you welcome me as your King?'

What an unexpected way to destroy all the works of the devil, not by force but with love. He came not with an army but with an invitation to be part of his new upside-down, inside-out kingdom that begins with the gift of a new heart.

'I will give you a new heart and put a new spirit in you;
I will remove from you your heart of stone and give you a heart of flesh.
And I will put my Spirit in you and move you to follow my decrees'
EZEKIEL 36:26–27

"Lord, I welcome you to be my King and I receive
your gift of a new heart. Fill me with your Spirit today."

THE KINGDOM SEED

You look for crowns and armies
I offer you a seed
A dull speck on your hand
Clutch it and it's worthless
Bury it with your ambition
And watch and wonder

How could this dot of greyness
Be leaf and branch
Burst to fragrant flower
And bend with golden fruit?

I offer you a seed
That you can cast aside
Or go down low and hide it in the earth
And watch it multiply.

GOD IS FOR YOU

Don't ever imagine that God stands by on the edge of the race of life with a critical eye. God is more like that embarrassing dad who comes to sports day and shouts louder than all the others. He is always cheering you on. If you fall down, he is there in a moment, ready to pick you up and set you back on your feet. When you are hurt, he will bandage you up. When you are gasping for breath because the race is long and hard, he will tell you to rest until you can get going again.

God is for you.

What, then, shall we say in response to these things? If God is for us, who can be against us? He who did not spare his own Son, but gave him up for us all – how will he not also, along with him, graciously give us all things?
ROMANS 8:31–32

Take some time to meditate on these verses and ask
God to show you that he is for you today.

The Lord

keeps you.

THE GIFT OF SECURITY

The shining blessing was first spoken over the people of Israel just after their great escape from Egypt as they faced the void ahead of them. Imagine them – a crowd of ex-slaves, probably still with whip-marks on their backs, treading tentatively towards a new future. They had left behind everything they knew and they had no idea where they were going. They desperately needed to hear that their all-powerful God was going to look after them.

We are not so different; even for us, life is more fragile than porcelain, more uncertain than the weather, and we are unable to control it, however hard we try. God wants us to have a deep sense of security that comes from hearing his promise to keep us. He is our all-powerful defender.

The Hebrew word for 'keep' is *shamar* which can also be translated 'guard, to watch for, to preserve or to tend'. It is the same word used in the book of Exodus when God reassures his precious people of his care,

'See, I am sending an angel ahead of you to guard you along the way'
EXODUS 23:20

Our God goes ahead of us. He went ahead of us through death to prepare a place for us and we can trust him to keep us on the journey.

 "Lord, I put my hand in yours today."

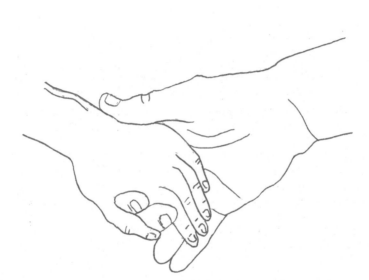

THE GIFT OF RELIANCE

Those first hearers of the blessing had no map. They had no directions. They weren't even sure where their next meal was coming from. At least in Egypt, they had been given slave-portions, definitely not gourmet but generally guaranteed. Life in the land of the Pharaohs had been hard, with far too many bricks to make, but at least they had known where they were going to sleep that night. Now they had to trust God for everything.

They might have escaped their slave masters but the future was hazy: they weren't yet in the Promised Land. They still had to take the territory. They faced an uncertain journey, an awful lot of hot sand and some bruising battles. They could only do it by total dependence on God.

Like them, we have not yet reached our Promised Land. We have been rescued by God from slavery to sin and death, but we have battles to fight if we are to see God's kingdom rule of love, justice and peace on earth. We too must completely rely on God.

In his kindness, God kept the Israelites; he led them and fed them every day. Jesus tells us to ask him every day for our daily bread. He asks us to fix our eyes on him, to trust him to keep us.

LORD, there is no one like you to
help the powerless against the mighty.
Help us, LORD our God, for we rely on you,
2 Chronicles 14:11

Consider what might stop you relying on God –
is it stubborn independence or pride or a lack of trust?

"Father, we praise you for there is none like you to
help the powerless; help us for we rely on you."

THE GIFT OF STRENGTH

The blessing is itself the power and strength for what is ahead.
As John Baillie prayed,

*I steadier step
When I recall
That though I slip
Thou dost not fall.*[3]

God's blessing is the power that enables us to run the great race. If you run a marathon, you can't run on empty. We can't do this Christian life on empty. Without the gift of security that this blessing brings, we will not stay the course. If I begin to think that God is not for me, I falter. I get scared to give because I need to hold onto my money. I fret about my looks or my qualifications or my reputation. I try and impress others when I forget that I am blessed. When I stop fuelling up on God's promises of blessing, I run out of steam; the tiniest rejections knock me off course and the big blows throw me down.

Today, will you deliberately draw your strength from his promise to keep you?

*The Sovereign LORD is my strength;
he makes my feet like the feet of a deer,
he enables me to tread on the heights.*

HABAKKUK 3:19

"Thank you Lord that your love is my security
and the strength of my heart."

KEPT THROUGH THE STORMS

The blessed life is not a trouble-free life lying back in the sunshine. We need a view of God's blessing that includes the storms. Storms were no surprise to Jesus. So much so that he could sleep through them! He expected trouble, without reading it as a sign of God's disfavour.

On one occasion, Jesus even sent his disciples ahead of him onto the lake into a storm. Mark tells us that the wind was against them and that 'they were making headway painfully' (Mark 6:48 ESV). That's an apt description of what life this side of heaven can sometimes feel like. They were exactly where Jesus had told them to go and still it was hard work.

The disciples obey Jesus and end up in a storm. Worse still, Jesus isn't in sight. But Mark tells us that Jesus sees them. Even when we can't see the Lord, he sees us. Difficulties do not mean that we are abandoned. The Lord comes to them in their trouble, walking on the water. It takes them a long time to recognize him. Maybe the waves were lashing and the spray was in their eyes; when life is toughest, it can be hard to see the Lord in the middle of the storm.

Initially, they cry out in terror but the Lord lovingly reassures them,

'Take heart; it is I. Do not be afraid.' (MARK 6:50 ESV)

Today the Lord says to you, 'Take heart, I'm here – don't be scared anymore.'

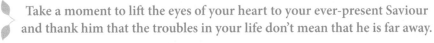

Take a moment to lift the eyes of your heart to your ever-present Saviour and thank him that the troubles in your life don't mean that he is far away.

THE GIFT OF A FAITHFUL FRIEND

When Joseph Scriven was in his early 20s, his fiancée drowned in an accident the day before his wedding. He emigrated from Ireland to Canada where he fell in love again, only to lose his second fiancée to illness. Yet Joseph ran to God and not away from him. He spent the remainder of his life giving away his time and his money to help those in need. He wrote a hymn which has helped so many through their times of trouble,

What a friend we have in Jesus, all our sins and griefs to bear.

Joseph understood that we are still on this side of heaven. We are not yet in the Promised Land; we are still in a broken, fallen world where tough things happen, but we have a Saviour who meets us here. We are not promised undiluted health and wealth; what we are promised is the presence of a Saviour who comes to be with us and who can bring good out of the worst circumstances.

When we bring them to him, our faithful friend 'will all our sorrows share'.

'When you go through deep waters, I will be with you.'
ISAIAH 43:2 NLT

Will you share your sorrows with him today?
"All my trust is in you, my most faithful of friends."

THE WINDOW OF HIS UNFAILING LOVE

Surprisingly, it is often those who have been through the toughest of times who most deeply grasp God's love for them. Elisabeth Elliot, whose husband was murdered by Auca Indians reportedly said,

We must view our circumstances through the window of God's love rather than viewing God's love through the window of our circumstances.

If I view God's nature through the window of my circumstances then I am floored by a bad headache or a broken computer, let alone a broken relationship or a serious medical diagnosis. If I view my circumstances through his love, everything changes.

Jesus never expected a trouble-free life. He expected the opposite: 'In this world you will have trouble.' But thank God, he didn't stop there. He went on,

'But take heart! I have overcome the world.'
JOHN 16:33

We often falter because we have a low expectation of trouble alongside a low expectation of blessing. The Bible calls us to have a high expectation of trouble and an *even higher* expectation of blessing.

 "Jesus, I bring all my circumstances beneath your unfailing love."

THE GIFT OF TRUTH

Stay alert! Watch out for your great enemy, the devil.
He prowls around like a roaring lion, looking for someone to devour.
1 PETER 5:8 NLT

We will be devoured if we fail to recognize that we have an enemy, the father of lies, who is always casting doubt on the goodness of God. In the creation story, the serpent suggests that the command not to eat from the tree is an expression of God's meanness; Satan still peddles the same lie, trying to convince us that God is not good.

When sorrows come, which they do, that's when we most need to remain in the truth of God's goodness. If we believe the filthy lie that God isn't good, then we will run away from him when we need him the most. God calls to us,

'Don't run away, run to me. Draw near, give me your sorrows, give me your deepest concerns and I will act on your behalf.'

"Father, keep us in your truth that you are good.
Today we lift high the name of Jesus, high over every demonic lie,
trusting in your unfailing love."

Knowing we belong

Before we can begin to grasp what it means for the Lord to keep us, we have to first know that we are his.

One day, an artist was robbed of his greatest masterpiece. Heartbroken, he trawled through galleries and auctions until he finally spotted it. It was wrecked, the frame split, the canvas scratched and torn. He spoke to the seller, 'That's mine – it was stolen!' The seller replied, 'Well, it's not yours now! You want it, you buy it!'

The artist emptied his bank account for this tattered, battered painting in order to call it his own again. Back home, he patiently and lovingly restored it.

To whom does the painting belong? The artist made, bought and restored it. It is his. This is the truth. You are God's: made, bought and being restored. You truly belong.

'The Lord knows those who are his,'
2 TIMOTHY 2:19

I am my beloved's and my beloved is mine;
SONG OF SOLOMON 6:3

 Slowly read that verse out several times and as you do so, give your heart again to the one who loves you best of all.

Treasured

Not only do we belong, we are treasured. In Exodus, God promises his people that if they obey him, they will be his treasured possession (Exodus 19:5).

What would you consider your most treasured possession? Not merely the most expensive but the most treasured? What would you give most to keep?

God faced the same question when our lives were captured by sin and responded by giving his life as the hostage ransom. You are worth the life of God. That's your price tag. That's what he paid to make you his own. He gave himself in Christ so that you could become his treasured possession.

'Finders keepers!' that's what God says over you. Whatever is ahead, God will keep you because you are his treasured possession, bought at an incalculable price. He will never let you go – not for all eternity.

'Don't be afraid, I've redeemed you.
I've called your name. You're mine.'
ISAIAH 43:1–2 MSG

God keeps you because he sees you as his treasure. How much do you think he values you?

 "Thank you for setting such a high price on my life. Thank you that I am your treasure."

LIFTING MY EYES TO THE ONE WHOSE EYES ARE ON ME

At times our faith can look like a flickering candle, vulnerable to a gust of cold wind. But just as Jesus prayed for the disciples that their faith would not fail, right now, he prays for us. At the Cross, it looked as if the disciples' faith had failed, but instead they turned out to be like those birthday candles that keep reigniting. Across the world, the persecuted church shows us that even in the face of the greatest suffering, Christianity reignites. God promises that when we call to him, he will keep us.

I lift up my eyes to the hills.
From where does my help come?
My help comes from the LORD,
who made heaven and earth.
He will not let your foot be moved;
he who keeps you will not slumber.

PSALM 121: 1–3 ESV

To what do you look for your security? Can you lift your eyes to God today?

Consider the fact that the Lord is constantly watching over you, the apple of his eye (Psalm 17:8). Is there a particular situation that you could entrust to God's keeping today?

 "Thank you Jesus that you are constantly watching over me, constantly praying for me. Keep me as the apple of your eye. I trust my life to your safekeeping today."

The Lord make his face shine on you

Blessed is the people of whom this is true;
blessed is the people whose God is the LORD.
Psalm 144:15

THE FATHER'S DELIGHT

Seven hundred years before Christ, Isaiah prophesied his coming as a beautiful sunrise shattering the darkness with glory,

'Arise, shine, for your light has come, and the glory of the LORD rises upon you.
See, darkness covers the earth and thick darkness is over the peoples,
but the LORD rises upon you and his glory appears over you.'

ISAIAH 60:1–2

God's face shines like the sun, brilliant in glory.

Yet God's shining face does not only reveal his glory, it is also a picture of his favour. Some commentators describe God's face shining upon us as his smile on us. Most of us don't have a clue how delighted God is to see us. Our heavenly Dad is like the father in the story of the Prodigal Son; he casts off all dignity, lifts up his robes and runs to meet us when we turn to him. As we lift our eyes, we find that his face is not dark with disapproval but lit up with joy.

Read the story of the Prodigal Son in Luke 15 and imagine yourself coming back to your Father. Can you see the delight on his face as he welcomes you back home?

A SON-RISE

The Bible tells the story of a hide-and-seek that is no game. If you wind back to the start, Adam and Eve are talking face-to-face with God, rejoicing in the blessing of God's face shining upon them. Then comes the saddest line in the Bible, 'Where are you?'

Adam hid because he had sinned. In our sin, we cannot look on God's face. That's why Isaiah laments, 'your sins have hidden his face from you,' (Isaiah 59:2). Yet God still longed to make his face shine upon us and so he gave the promise of a new sunrise in the birth of his Son. Such is the tender mercy of our God,

by which the rising sun will come to us from heaven
to shine on those living in darkness
and in the shadow of death,
LUKE 1:78–79

When the sun rises, grey is banished by colour and all is made new.

 "Thank you Jesus that you light up our darkness and dispel every shadow."

THE TORN CURTAIN

In the Old Testament, the towering curtain in the temple hid God not because God needs protecting but because we do. Only one man once a year could enter the Most Holy Place where God dwelt and that was only after a sacrifice for sin had been made. How could the rest of us see God's shining face? How could we know his favour?

Jesus changed everything.

At Jesus' birth, the angels sang, 'on earth peace to those on whom his favour rests' (Luke 2:14).

At Jesus' death, that curtain in the temple was ripped from top to bottom.

Through Jesus' resurrection, we are raised up to new life.

'But for you who revere my name, the sun of righteousness will rise with healing in its rays.'
MALACHI 4:2

"Father, I praise you with all of my heart that nothing can separate me from your love today. I can live in your favour, in the light of your shining face."

The Searcher

Immensity packed down
Into a teenage womb
How can this be?
Try stuffing stars into a suitcase
Or pocketing the moon!
How can the maker of it all become as small as you and me?

Stripped of your glory
You entered my story
The author came to make it his own
You stooped down
To scoop me up
With your fortress-breaking, heart re-making, nail-pierced human hands
I thought I was boldly searching
Instead I have been found
By your wonder of wonders
Love[4]

THE GLORY OF GOD
IN THE FACE OF CHRIST

Whom no senses can reveal
Was for us made manifest
IGNATIUS C. 105 AD

After three years with Jesus, Philip says to him, 'Lord, show us the Father and that will be enough for us.' Jesus answers,

'Don't you know me, Philip, even after I have been among you
such a long time? Anyone who has seen me has seen the Father.
How can you say, "Show us the Father"?'
JOHN 14:8–9

What a statement! Jesus clearly claims to be God's shining face.

We can see the face of God in Christ and it is always more wonderful than we expected. Jesus likes prayer and parties and picnics on the beach. He cares for the poor and touches the untouchable. He makes friends with fraudsters and prostitutes and intellectuals. He is constantly surprising – to the point of raising the dead. He shows us what God is like.

The Son is the radiance of God's glory
HEBREWS 1:3

How can we see that shining face today? God has given us not only his Word but also his Spirit so that daily we can meet with him.

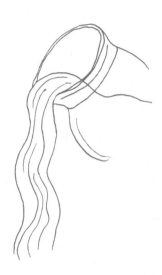

'I will no longer hide my face from them,
for I will pour out my Spirit on the people of Israel,
declares the Sovereign LORD.'
EZEKIEL 39:29

Think about what you love about Jesus.
Praise God – that's what he is like.

THE GIFT OF REVELATION

Our God longs to make himself known to us.

No one has ever seen God, but the one and only Son … has made him known.
JOHN 1:18

C. S. Lewis has the senior demon in *The Screwtape Letters* writing in exasperation about God,

'To human animals on their knees, He pours out self-knowledge in a quite shameless fashion.'[5]

The key phrase there is 'on our knees'. Perhaps it is time we acknowledged that we cannot find God on our own. Iranaeus wrote in the second century that only God can reveal God to us. How did we ever think we could get our little minds around the maker of the universe? As if an ant could access the internet or a microbe could map the stars.

We cannot find him on our own so thank God that he searches tirelessly for those who seek after him. He promises,

'You will seek me and find me when you seek me with all your heart.'
JEREMIAH 29:13

If you can, kneel down before God and tell him that you are seeking him. If you are unable to physically do it, you can make it the attitude of your heart. Thank him for his promise to make himself known to you.

GOD SAYS, 'SEEK MY FACE!'

Jesus began his guide to blessing in Matthew 5 by stirring up our desire for more; he shows us that blessing starts with acknowledging our need, by being hungry, thirsty and poor.

'Blessed are the poor in spirit, for theirs is the kingdom of heaven.
Blessed are those who mourn, for they will be comforted.
Blessed are the meek, for they will inherit the earth.
Blessed are those who hunger and thirst for righteousness, for they will be filled.'
MATTHEW 5:3–6

Trust God that the thirst that drew you to read this book is a sign that you are blessed by him. As we connect with our desperate desire to see his face, then we are blessed.

We pray with Augustine,

Lord, put salt on our lips that we may thirst for you.

Here is a prayer that we know God loves to answer. God tells us to seek his face because he longs to make it shine upon us.
'Jesus, joy of man's desiring' waits to be found by us.[6]

 "Father, you tell us to seek your face because you long to make it shine upon us. Make me thirsty for you today."

49

SETTING BLESSING HIGHEST

'I will not let you go unless you bless me.'
Jacob
GENESIS 32:26

It appears that God's top criterion for blessing is an eagerness to go after it. Why else would God choose to show his face to Jacob of all people? Jacob, the cheat. Jacob, the liar. Jacob, the thief. His name means 'grasper' and he lives up to it. He didn't just steal from strangers, he conned his way into his brother's inheritance.

God showed his face to Jacob because Jacob set blessing above everything else. His methods were terrible, involving conniving, scheming and fancy dress, but, in the end, Jacob is exalted over his brother Esau. All because Jacob valued the Father's blessing while Esau despised it. Esau was prepared to sell off his right to his father's blessing for a bowl of stew. What a warning for us who are too quickly tempted to exchange an eternity of the Father's blessing for a few material advantages here.

It is easily done. Esau looks like a fool to hand over his inheritance to quieten his rumbling tummy, but how often is that scene replayed? Except that the bowl of stew is a brief affair or a dodgy contract at work or even the apparently legitimate distractions of education or ambition or romance. I wonder what distracts you from setting blessing highest?

What can I do to chase after the Father's blessing on my life?

The wrestle

Jacob wrestled all night with a stranger, refusing to let go until his opponent gave him a blessing. God is looking for those who will grip on to him until they are blessed. Apart from sexual intimacy or a hug, wrestling is as close as we get to someone else. That's why boys love wrestling matches with their dads and rugby scrums. Maybe that's one reason God sometimes makes us wrestle with him; he so desperately wants us near.

Jacob is prepared to get up close and personal with God, chest to chest, sweaty hands, a strange embrace but nonetheless, an embrace. God wants to embrace us and Jacob wins the blessing because he is prepared to come close to this God who is looking for those who dare to draw near. For all his faults, Jacob is not passive; he believes there is more to be had and so Jacob wrestles and Jacob has an encounter with his maker.

"Father God, I praise you with all of my heart.
When I draw close to you, you always come close to me.
Today I hold on to the one who holds onto me,
trusting your promise to abundantly bless me."

THE WAIT

I press on to take hold of that for which Christ Jesus took hold of me.
PHILIPPIANS 3:12

God is evidently not a fan of instant gratification. Why is that? Is it because the wrestle for blessing is the furnace that purifies our hearts? It's often in the wrestling that he strips away our false motives and we come to recognize that he is truly our heart's desire.

The bigger the blessing, the bigger the battle before it. We have to press on and press in to win the prize. Look at Abraham, promised a nation of descendants, waiting and waiting in the desert. Look at Joseph, waiting for his dream, languishing in a foreign dungeon. Look at David, spending years on the run, waiting to become king. Look at Mary, still waiting for her promised son to become the Messiah as she stared at a cross. Again and again, in the lives of the great biblical heroes, dreams are delayed and promises precede testing.

Seeking and waiting often go together.
But with God, waiting time is never wasted time.
Are you waiting? Be strong, take heart and wait for the Lord.

OVERCOMERS

To our surprise, Jacob wins a wrestling match with God! He is told,

'Your name will no longer be Jacob, but Israel, because you have struggled with God and with humans and have overcome.'

GENESIS 32:28

Looking closely, it's clear that the divine stranger had the winning move, crippling Jacob, yet Jacob is described as the winner because he would not let go without a blessing.

How could Jacob overcome God? That's like a toddler taking on a Sumo wrestler. Jacob knew that he was the weaker wrestler because afterwards he says, 'I saw God face to face, and yet my life was spared' (Genesis 32:30).

Jacob overcame only because God wanted him to. God so longed to bless Jacob that he allowed himself to be overcome in a wrestling match. That same God so longs to bless us that he allowed himself to be overcome on a cross to make us overcomers.

 "I praise you Jesus, Lord of the Universe, that you were overcome on that Cross to make me an overcomer today."

Seeking not striving

Do not strive in your own strength; cast yourself at the feet of the Lord Jesus,
and wait upon Him in the sure confidence that He is with you, and works in you.[7]
ANDREW MURRAY

Wrestling for blessing is not striving. We don't wrestle to earn God's favour but rather because we are pressing in to claim what is promised. This isn't about twisting God's arm with our determination; blessing is always a gift of grace.

My husband described seeking God as putting yourself in the way of grace. Years ago, Trevor took a day to pray. He sat beside a stream and his attention was caught by the smooth shining stones in the flow of the water. They could not have been more different to the ones on the bank which were jagged, dark and grimy.

How do we put our lives in the stream of God's grace? This is where spiritual disciplines come in – Bible reading and prayer, silence and celebration, meditation and giving, fasting and solitude – to name but a few.[8] These can all be ways of immersing ourselves in God.

We are invited to encounter the only one from whom all blessings flow.

 "Lord help me to daily place myself in the endless stream of your grace."

SHINING FACES

It doesn't end with God's face shining on us. He makes his light shine in us.

God, who said, 'Let light shine out of darkness,' made his light shine in our hearts
to give us the light of the knowledge of God's glory displayed in the face of Christ.
2 CORINTHIANS 4:6

When Moses gazed on the face of God, his face shone. So too for us.

We all, who with unveiled faces contemplate the Lord's glory,
are being transformed into his image with ever-increasing glory,
which comes from the Lord, who is the Spirit.
2 CORINTHIANS 3:18

We don't have to be overwhelmed by the darkness in our world. God has long
planned that the light of his salvation would reach to the ends of the earth –
through us!

'Arise, shine, for your light has come, and the glory of the LORD rises upon you!'
ISAIAH 60:1

"Father, make your light shine in my heart today.
May your glory of Christ shine through my prayers,
my words and my deeds."

CLAY POTS

Just a handful of Christians stood against Nazism. One was Bonhoeffer who said this: 'the flight into the invisible is a denial of the call of God.'[9]

Why do we so often fly into the invisible with our fingers in our ears denying the call of God? Is it fear, is it selfishness, is it just more comfortable hiding in the shadows? Is it that we don't feel very shiny? Our lives look more cracked and scuffed than glorious.

Paul says we are like frail, cracked clay jars BUT God has still placed his treasure in us – the treasure of *the light of the knowledge of the glory of God in the face of Christ.* That makes us richer than Solomon, the Queen and Bill Gates all rolled together.

Imagine someone offered you a cheque for a million, would you care if the envelope was grubby? We might feel like that grubby envelope when it comes to sharing our faith but the point is that the treasure we offer is priceless.

The man first chosen to pronounce our shining blessing was far from perfect. It was Aaron! Aaron who had made the golden calf. Aaron the faithless. How encouraging – we never have to *be* the source of blessing, just the mouthpiece. All the saving power, all the blessing comes from God. We are simply the clay pots.

Those who look to him are radiant; their faces are never covered with shame.

PSALM 34:5

 "Thank you Father that I can look to you and be radiant today."

The Lord

be gracious to you

RECEIVE

The way to the blessed Christian life is receiving all that God wants to give us. Paul explains that those who reign in life are those who *receive* the abundance of God's grace (Romans 5:17).

Repentance is God's kind gift to clear the darkness that hides his shining face, but it is a gift that needs to be received.

I said, 'I will confess my transgressions to the Lord.'
And you forgave the guilt of my sin.
PSALM 32:5

What a tragedy if we confess our sins but never go on to trust that God has forgiven us and so we lose the joy of our salvation.

 "Father, I receive the costly gift of your forgiveness today."

REPENTANCE BRINGS JOY!

Biblical repentance is not empty regret – in Hebrew the word literally means 'returning'. The gospel is God's call for us to return home to the Father, to joy.

Jesus gives us the best explanation of repentance by telling a story. In Luke 15, Jesus describes a rebellious young man who rejects his dad to live wild and free in a far-off land, except that the wildness and freedom turns out to be poverty and isolation. Riches spent, he ends up in a pigsty, spiritually and physically unclean. Finally, at rock bottom, he remembers how good life was with his father and returns home.

The result is the most amazing party, a celebration, an explosion of the father's joy over his son. It is a joy echoed in the story of the good shepherd bringing home the lost sheep.

he joyfully puts it on his shoulders and goes home. Then he calls his friends and neighbours together and says, "Rejoice with me; I have found my lost sheep."

LUKE 15:5–6

 "Father, help me see your joy over me today."

SEEING THE FATHER'S GOODNESS

In Jesus' story in Luke 15, the turning point comes when the young man *remembers* how good his father is.

Evagrius, the fourth-century monk, said, 'Sin is forgetfulness of the goodness of God.' When I head off in my own direction, I am denying that God has the best for me. Sin's subtext is that God is not truly good; when we sin, we deny that God's ways are best for us. In contrast, true repentance always reasserts the goodness of God. That's why the New Testament Greek word for repentance, *metanoia*, means a change of mind.

This is a million miles away from the negative view of repentance that prevails. It's not just empty regret. It is a whole new way of thinking about God and about life. If I know that God is God and that he is good and he is for me, then no sin pattern can grip me. Despair is dispelled. Repentance is not self-pity, a wallowing in sadness over sin, but a triumphant and joyful renunciation of sin in the power of the risen Christ.

It is in repentance that the encounter takes place between grace and freedom.
FATHER RANIERO CANTALAMESSA

 Do I need to remember how good my heavenly Father is?

Resisting the accuser

Too many Christians live life with a vague sense of having disappointed God. But Jesus went to the Cross so that we would not have to feel guilty. Instead of living life with guilt snapping at your heels, how about facing it head on with the question, 'Is there any sin pattern in my life that I need to repent of?' When we know that God is utterly good and on our side, it is not as hard as it may sound. Ask God to search your heart. As we bring our lives into the light of his word, he shows us specifically where we need to change. Vague guilt is never from him and we have authority from God to dismiss every accusing lie.

When we struggle, we don't have to battle alone. Find a mature Christian you can trust. Bonhoeffer wrote, 'In the presence of a psychiatrist, I can only be a sick man. In the presence of another Christian, I can dare to be a sinner.'[10]

Confess your sins to each other and pray for each other so that you may be healed.
JAMES 5:16

Search me, God, and know my heart …
PSALM 139:23

MORE GRACE

Often our temptation is to elevate our weaknesses above grace; God calls us to elevate his grace and love above all else. God says to us today,

'My grace is sufficient for you,
for my power is made perfect in weakness.'

2 CORINTHIANS 12:9

Give yourself fully to God.
He will use you to accomplish great things
on the condition that you believe much more in
his love than your own weakness.

MOTHER TERESA

Grace is always more
More than debts paid for, grace enriches me
More than my striving, grace empowers me
More than my fears, grace emboldens me
More than my aspirations, grace surprises me
Grace is always more.

By grace not my effort

To live the blessed life, we have to abandon our feeble attempts at self-justification. We cannot earn blessing. As if we could ever justify ourselves before God! Paul is succinct about the problem: *'Cursed is everyone who does not do everything written in the law' (Galatians 3:10)* – that definitely includes you and me.

What a relief that Paul does not end there but explains how Christ rescued us. On the Cross, God took the curse so that we might be blessed.

Christ redeemed us from the curse of the law
… in order that the blessing given to Abraham might come to the Gentiles …
GALATIANS 3:12–14

 "Father, I am sorry for all the times that I try to justify myself. Thank you that I can hand all that over to you in exchange for your wonderful blessing."

THE GIFT OF RIGHTEOUSNESS

What is this blessing that we inherit through Abraham? First of all, Abraham was given righteousness. Although a sinner, because Abraham believed, righteousness was *credited* to him. When it comes to righteousness, we have all exceeded our overdraft facility. Yet God moves us from the debit to the credit column.[11]

Before any other blessing, we need this gift of right-standing with God. It is the foundation for all other blessings. As Terry Virgo explains, in his wonderful book, *God's Lavish Grace*, it's like painting a watercolour. If you don't allow the first layer to dry, you end up with a blurry mess.[12] If you try to earn God's blessing by keeping the law, you end up back in the place of the curse. You don't need a way to The Way.

God made him who had no sin to be sin for us, so that in him we might become the righteousness of God.
2 CORINTHIANS 5:21

"Father God, thank you that you welcome me into your presence to exchange the filthy rags of my own righteousness for the clean white clothing of the righteousness of Christ."

RECEIVING LIKE A CHILD

'Truly I tell you, anyone who will not receive the kingdom of God like a little child will never enter it.' And he took the children in his arms, placed his hands on them and blessed them.'

MARK 10:15–16

To be blessed, we have to be childlike. What are children like?

Children are good at asking. James says,
'You do not have because you do not ask God' (James 4:2).

Children are good at receiving. Just watch them at Christmas.
What does God want to give you today?

Children are trusting. Tell God today, 'I trust in your unfailing love;' (Psalm 13:5).

Children are also messy! Jesus lived in a peasant community where children probably had drippy noses and grubby clothes. He still gathered them in his arms. We don't have to clean up before we come to God. We can come to God as we are.

God demonstrates his own love for us in this:
while we were still sinners, Christ died for us.

ROMANS 5:8

 "Jesus, take me in your arms and bless me.
I put my trust in your unfailing love."

THE BLESSING OF THE HOLY SPIRIT

God's grace is such that we are not only given right-standing with God but given power to live righteously by his Holy Spirit. I am not only given grace; I am empowered to give grace to others.

He redeemed us in order that the blessing given to Abraham
might come to the Gentiles through Christ Jesus,
*so that **by faith** we might receive the promise of the Spirit.*
GALATIANS 3:14

This is the most precious gift of all, the greatest blessing and the way to blessing – *God gives us himself.*

In response, we have to trust that this gift is indeed a gift and grab it with both hands. In Hebrews 11:17, we are told that Abraham *embraced* the promises. Will you embrace the promise of the Spirit today?

"Thank you Father for the precious
gift of yourself in your Spirit."

MORE OF GOD

We have everything in Christ. There is no more to be given but more to be taken.

God has so much more of himself to give to us.

*'If you then, though you are evil, know how to give good gifts to your children,
how much **more** will your Father in heaven give the Holy Spirit to those who ask him!'*
LUKE 11:13

God always says yes to that prayer. Whether we hear the heavens boom or
whether we simply hear his gentle whisper, Jesus is to be trusted when he says,

*'Whoever believes in me, as the Scripture has said,
"Out of his heart will flow rivers of living water."'*
JOHN 7:38 ESV

Streams of water and springs of water are different to pools in that they flow.
What matters is that we daily invite a steady stream of the presence of the
living God into our lives.

Father God, fill me again
that I may know you more clearly,
love you more dearly,
and follow you more nearly.[13]

The Lord

turn his face
towards you

THE GIFT OF ATTENTION

Love pays attention. Marriages falter when couples ignore each other. Children play up when their parents are too busy to notice them. How wonderful that our blessing promises us the most profound connection of all – with God himself. He turns his face towards us. He pays us attention.

The original Hebrew is sometimes translated 'May Yahweh lift up his face toward you'. It is the opposite of the proverbial cold shoulder. This is an invitation to deep friendship with God. We are told of Moses,

The LORD would speak to Moses face to face, as one speaks to a friend.
EXODUS 33:11

It seems outrageously presumptuous to imagine that we could be invited that near to God, but Jesus himself says 'I have called you friends,' (John 15:15). It changes everything when I know that the eyes of the Most High are watching me with love.

 "Father, may I live today as a friend of God, knowing that you watch me with great love."

THE GIFT OF RECONCILIATION

He who cannot forgive breaks the bridge over which he himself must pass.
GEORGE HERBERT

Here comes the challenge. We can cut ourselves off from the blessing of knowing God face to face. The Bible is clear that if you refuse to forgive others, you exclude yourself from this blessing. It's like hiding in a hovel that shuts out the sunlight.

It is a mistake to think that God's grace comes without conditions. God's love is totally unconditional; he loves you as much when you are jealous and greedy as when you are helping the homeless. However, we cannot reach out to receive that love if our hands are clutching onto grudges.

Jesus puts a big conditional 'if' in front of his promise of the blessing of forgiveness, saying, 'if you do not forgive others their sins, your Father will not forgive your sins' (Matthew 6:15).

Reconciliation is not an optional extra to God; it is in the centre of his loving nature to be a reconciler. The God who turns his face towards us calls us to do the same.

 Is there someone you need to forgive today?

BLESSED ARE THE PEACEMAKERS

To forgive is to set a prisoner free
and discover that the prisoner was you.[14]

LEWIS B. SMEDES

The story of Jacob vividly illustrates the link between blessing and forgiveness. In Genesis 32, Jacob encounters God in his wrestling match and says, 'I have met God face to face'. The following day, Jacob is reconciled with his brother Esau and makes this astounding statement: 'to see your face is like seeing the face of God, now that you have received me favourably' (Genesis 33:10).

Jacob knew what God's face looked like and then said that reconciliation with his brother was like seeing the face of God! The implication for us is clear – a life of forgiveness is essential to living in the blessing of God's shining face.

If you know that you harbour bitterness, ask the Lord to help you.
In the quietness of your room, speak out forgiveness to the one
who has wounded you and pray a blessing on them. If that's too hard,
find someone to pray with about it.

THE GIFT OF A BROKEN AND CONTRITE HEART

Luke tells the story of a supper party (Luke 7:36) which begins with the host, Simon, failing to wash the feet of Jesus. It was a shocking omission. Simon was publically humiliating Jesus.

Then the gatecrasher arrives, simply described as a sinful woman. She washes Jesus' feet with her tears, dries them with her hair and cracks open her valuable jar of perfume for him. This is adoration.

Has your heart ever been broken before God like hers? She didn't just break the jar of perfume; the hard layer around her heart was so utterly shattered that when she knelt at Jesus' feet, she began to sob. Why did she love Jesus so much? Jesus says, 'whoever has been forgiven little loves little' (Luke 7:47). It was because this woman had been forgiven much that she loved much.

Ultimately our love is the one thing that matters (Luke 10:27). What God wants from us is our love for eternity. Yet our love can grow cold, almost without noticing. I can be like Simon; I may invite Jesus into my house, but actually be testing him, not really welcoming him and shutting off my heart from him. Or I can give myself in adoration to the one who turned his face to me with such grace.

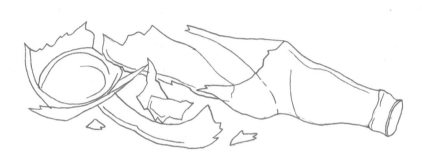

"Jesus, may I pour out my love on you today."

The gift of holiness

'I am the LORD who makes you holy.'
LEVITICUS 20:8

Like us, the sinful woman is only beginning to realize the magnitude of the forgiveness offered in Christ. She has discovered enough of Jesus' forgiveness to fall at his feet but she still carries too much shame to come face to face with him – she sidles up behind Jesus to pour perfume upon him.

Jesus doesn't let her hide. He wants to turn his face towards her. He calls her out and says 'Your sins are forgiven'. She had flagrantly broken his law and yet he publically declares her forgiveness. What a moment! Simon judges her as unclean, exiled from God but she finds that God's face is turned to her in Jesus. Jesus' forgiveness was greater than her unholiness. Simon thought that the touch of a woman like that would defile him but when she touched Jesus, he made her holy rather than her making him unclean. No wonder she wept as a lifetime of shame was lifted.

Simon missed the forgiveness of Jesus because he was so busy taking the role of judge and jury. He passed judgement first on Jesus and then on the woman. Who will we be like? The 'sinful woman', forgiven and adoring, or Simon, judging and judged? He thought he was holy and overlooked the holy one who could make him holy.

Jesus speaks over you today, 'Your sins are forgiven'.
How will you respond to the one who makes you holy?

WHAT FORGIVENESS ISN'T

Forgiveness isn't unfair because ultimately everyone will face God. Only God knows the full picture and only God can judge truly,

Do not take revenge, my dear friends, but leave room for God's wrath, for it is written: 'It is mine to avenge; I will repay,' says the Lord. On the contrary: 'If your enemy is hungry, feed him; if he is thirsty, give him something to drink. In doing this, you will heap burning coals on his head.'

ROMANS 12:19—20

Forgiveness isn't denying the hurt. Desmond Tutu, who led the post-apartheid Truth and Reconciliation Commission in South Africa, put it beautifully,

[Forgiveness] means taking what happened seriously but drawing out the sting in the memory. [15]

Forgiveness isn't being a doormat. Forgiveness isn't being trampled on or remaining mute in conflict situations.

Forgiveness isn't dependent on feelings. I don't wait to forgive until I feel forgiving or I may wait a long time. Forgiveness is always a choice, one that we may have to make over and over again.

 Because nothing is impossible with God, it will never be impossible to forgive.

FORGIVENESS — A PATHWAY TO BLESSING

Do not repay evil with evil or insult with insult, but with blessing,
... that you may inherit a blessing.

1 PETER 3:9

I can release the debts that others owe me because I am rich in Christ. I don't have to draw on my meagre reserves but can forgive from the place of being profoundly loved and comforted by God. I can trust his promise that all can be redeemed and God can turn to good what Satan intended for evil.

The Lord who turns his face towards us calls us to turn our faces towards those who have hurt or wounded us. What does that look like for you today?

"Forgive us as we forgive those who sin against us."

The Lord

give you
his peace

GOD'S GIFT OF PEACE

You will keep in perfect peace
those whose minds are steadfast,
because they trust in you.
ISAIAH 26:3

God's gift of peace to us, the grand finale of the blessing, is his restoration of all the shalom, of all the well-being, that God originally intended for us. When God offers us his peace, he is promising something more than an escape, more than the end of conflict, more than an absence of noise and more than removal of stress. Appealing as all of those are, a definition by negatives is still a diminished view of peace. God's peace, his shalom is far richer.

Shalom ... is the way things ought to be.[16]
CORNELIUS PLANTINGA, JR

I rest beneath the Almighty's shade,
My griefs expire, my troubles cease;
Thou, Lord, on whom my soul is stayed,
Wilt keep me still in perfect peace.
CHARLES WESLEY

THE GIFT OF 'GOD WITH US'

This is the great Christian story:

Creation: God walks with Adam and Eve.

Incarnation: God leaves the glory of heaven to
become our Immanuel which means 'God with us'.

Crucifixion: The Cross shouts out, 'God wants to be with you'.

Resurrection: The risen Jesus appears saying,
'surely I am with you always,' (Matthew 28:20).

Pentecost: God pours out his Holy Spirit – his presence with us forever.

The Wedding Feast: The Bride is united with her bridegroom forever.

 "Thank you Father, Son and Spirit that you want to be with me."

87

GOD HIMSELF IS PEACE

Peace is a person. God reveals himself to Gideon as Yahweh-Shalom, which means 'The LORD is Peace' (Judges 6:24). This is wonderful – God does not only give us the attribute of peace; he himself is our peace.

Jesus' final words in Matthew 28 are 'I am with you always', or as Bruner paraphrases,

Look! I myself am right there with you every single day of your life, even if you don't realize it. [17]

What could be a greater foundation for our security than knowing that God is with us? With us is the one with all authority, who overcame death and hell and Satan and sin! And he isn't a passive passenger, just coming along for the ride. God is for us - at our side and on our side.

Is there some way that you can remind yourself throughout today that God is with you and for you?

"I will fear no evil for you are with me!"

PSALM 23:4

THE GIFT OF REASSURANCE

What about when we doubt? God is so kind when we question him. When John the Baptist ends up on death row, he sends Jesus a message asking The Big Question, *'Are you really the promised Saviour?'* John had been there when God spoke from heaven declaring Jesus to be his beloved Son. Yet Jesus doesn't rebuke John for unbelief, but instead reassures him; he sends the disciples to tell John all the wonderful things that they have seen Jesus do and say.

Jesus challenges willful unbelief but never rejects his disciples for doubting. Instead, the risen Saviour comes to doubting Thomas and says, 'Peace be with you!' (John 20:26).

Today he wants us to focus on his faithfulness rather than on our wavering faith.

 "Thank you Lord that even when I am faithless, you remain faithful, for you cannot disown yourself."
2 TIMOTHY 2:13

THE GIFT OF REMEMBRANCE

The more we seek God, the more we see him work. Then we can grow our own faith history to hold onto when we struggle. After winning a fierce battle, Samuel set up a big stone, calling it Ebenezer, which means 'God has helped us get this far' (1 Samuel 7:12). You probably won't set up a big stone pillar in your garden, but what might help you remember *what the Lord has done for you?*

Every January, I make an Ebenezer list of what God has done for me the year before. It is deeply encouraging. I need it because it's easy to ignore God's help. Every breath comes from him. Every good gift is from above, but too quickly we forget the giver.

 Think about this last week; can you see one way that God helped you that you hadn't even noticed? What are the 'I am with you' reminders that God is sending you?

The gift of unity

When Christians are in conflict with one another, they make Christ's body suffer. [18]
POPE FRANCIS

There is no peace without unity. That's why Paul wrote to Philippi urging the Christians there to 'agree in the Lord'. God commands us to make every effort to be united (Philippians 4:2, ESV; Ephesians 4:3).

Unity costs; it is hard to lay down the desire to be vindicated. It goes against our selfishness to make Jesus central. But the prize of unity is a million times worth the cost,

For there the LORD bestows his blessing,
even life for evermore.
PSALM 133:3

"Father, make us one."

THE GIFT OF CONTENTMENT

I have learned the secret of being content in any and every situation,
GALATIANS 4:12

Even in a prison cell! Paul wrote these words, whilst under arrest, with
the prospect of martyrdom on the horizon. Yet he didn't think that his
circumstances needed to change for him to be content. He didn't give ground
to the envy that erodes peace like bone cancer.

How encouraging that Paul *learned* the secret of contentment! Contentment
isn't something we either have or don't have – we can learn it. We can *un*learn
the twisted values of our culture that say 'I need more' or 'this situation must
change before I can be content'. We can learn to find our contentment in Christ.

Father help me find my
deepest joy in you today.
May I see all I have in Christ.

THE GIFT OF PRAYER

A prayerless Christian is like a bus driver trying alone to push his bus out of a rut because he doesn't know Clark Kent is on board.[19]

JOHN PIPER

Going solo is foolish. God has given us the gift of prayer.

Does praying sound harder than worrying? Some people think that prayer is an inbuilt talent possessed by elite spiritual heavyweights. In fact, all God wants is for you to bring him the honest cry of your heart. You don't have to be eloquent, just real.

The LORD is near to all who call on him,

PSALM 145:18

So don't worry – pray! The one who cares enough to make the daffodils dance in the wind to delight you, who painted a butterfly's wings to make your heart sing, won't he care for you?

Is there a situation you can hand over to your loving Father today?

THE GIFT OF THANKFULNESS

The Lord is near. Do not be anxious about anything, but in everything, by prayer and petition, with thanksgiving, present your requests to God.
PHILIPPIANS 4:5–6

Paul doesn't just say 'Don't worry'; he presents us with an alternative – thankful prayer. It's much easier not to think of a squirrel when you think of a duck and it is easier not to worry when you are being thankful.

Thankfulness magnifies God and that resizes our anxieties. When we put the Creator of the universe in the picture, he is always bigger.

When you look at the world, you get distressed,
when you look inward, you get depressed,
but when you look upwards, you find rest.
CORRIE TEN BOOM

 What can you thank God for today?

The gift of Joy

Joy is a command. It's not a suggestion; it's an imperative,
'Rejoice in the Lord!'[20]

Does that mean tripping through life with a fake smile through gritted teeth?
In a fallen world, there are times to mourn. Jesus wept for his friend Lazarus
even though he knew that he would raise Lazarus in the end. But Jesus set
joy before him to enable him to persevere. Wonderfully, the joy he saw at the
finish line was gathering you and me into his arms. We too can know that the
final chapter of our story is joy. Not just a drizzle but a torrent of joy that will
never end.

The promise is that joy will win the race,

and those the LORD has rescued will return.
They will enter Zion with singing;
everlasting joy will crown their heads.
Gladness and joy will overtake them,
and sorrow and sighing will flee away.
ISAIAH 35:10

 "Lord, we rejoice in you."

THE GIFT OF PURPOSE

Recognizing that God has a purpose for us is the decisive blow to discontentment that robs us of *shalom*. Satan is desperate to convince us that we are irrelevant but if we believe that, we won't do the little things that make the big difference. Imagine if the boy with loaves and fishes had thought that, he would have missed out on a miracle.

Paul's guide to *shalom* in Philippians 4:9 says,

Whatever you have learned or received or heard from me,
or seen in me – put it into practice.
And the God of peace will be with you.

God designed us to put his word into practice and to make a tangible difference in our world.

"Father, please show me how I can put
your word into practice in my life.
Make me a blessing today."

A New Name

"The LORD bless you and keep you
The LORD make his face shine on you and be gracious to you;
the LORD turn his face towards you
and give you peace."
'So they will put my name on the Israelites, and I will bless them.'

The final goal

'So they will put my name on the Israelites, and I will bless them.'
NUMBERS 6:27

We mustn't miss the last act of the play. The blessing ends with the most precious of promises – that we would bear the name of God. It is a promise that weaves right through Scripture until the day when blessing finally, completely overcomes the curse,

No longer will there be any curse.
The throne of God and of the Lamb will be in the city,
and his servants will serve him.
They will see his face,
and his name will be on their foreheads.
REVELATION 22:3–4

Praise God that this is the end of our story.

WHAT DOES IT LOOK LIKE FOR US TO BEAR THE NAME OF GOD?

Firstly, name-bearing speaks of belonging. God names us as his own. He writes his name on us with an indelible pen that says that we belong to him; we are his people called by his name. But there is yet more to bearing the name of God – bearing God's name is about becoming like him. Because God's name reveals his character, bearing his name means wearing his character – which is compassionate and gracious, slow to anger, abounding in love and faithfulness (Exodus 34).

How wonderful that he puts his name on us through blessing us! That's why God gives Aaron the shining blessing and then explains, 'So they will put my name on the Israelites' (Numbers 6:27).

 Spend some time praying over these words: compassionate and gracious, slow to anger, abounding in love and faithfulness.

THE PROMISE OF TRANSFORMATION

With Jesus, we are not just learning how to 'do' what he does, we are learning how to be like him. It is not just skills that we are picking up, but it is that we are transformed on the inside to have his character and his mind as well.[21]

The Father is conforming us to the image of his Son (Romans 8:29).

Every Christian is to become a little Christ. The whole purpose of becoming a Christian is simply nothing else.[22]

C. S. LEWIS

All of life becomes a school of transformation; every moment an opportunity for the great artist to restore his image in us. As John Stott wrote,

Christlikeness is the purpose of God for the people of God.[23]

 "Father, please send your Spirit and make me like Christ."

THE GIFT OF AN EASY YOKE

At the time of Jesus, people understood that the aim of a disciple was to become like their teacher. It was said that they did this by coming *under the yoke* of their rabbi's teaching.

Jesus would have regularly seen oxen with wooden yokes, pulling heavy carts. Maybe he spent long hours smoothing rough wood to make a light well-fitted yoke. He reassures us that his teaching is not too hard for us,

'For my yoke is easy and my burden is light.'
MATTHEW 11:30

God has designed a perfectly-fitted yoke of truth to help us carry every weight that life brings. Unlike the rabbis who gave their disciples lengthy lists of rules without lifting a finger to help them, Jesus says,

'Take my yoke upon you and learn from me, for I am gentle and humble in heart, and you will find rest for your souls.'
MATTHEW 11:29

 Can you hear him calling you to be his disciple today?

THE YOKE IS CROSS-SHAPED

The call to discipleship is the call to follow Christ ... all the way to the Cross.

*'Whoever wants to be my disciple must deny themselves
and take up their cross and follow me.'*
MATTHEW 16:24

So much of our culture is about self-realization, that the call to the Cross jars. Perhaps it always did. When Peter heard Jesus talking about dying, he rebuked his teacher. Yet even the teaching about the Cross is part of the easy yoke. How? Because Calvary is where every enslaving yoke is broken, Calvary is where the tyranny of self is defeated, Calvary is where guilt is banished and Calvary is where I am made free.

 "Jesus, how can I ever thank you for taking the path to the Cross so that I can follow you there to freedom?!"

THE RADICAL SOLUTION

At the time of Jesus, if you saw anyone carrying their cross, you knew why –
they were going to die. God's solution to our deepest problems is radical – 'Die!'

Here is life-changing power:

We know that our old self was crucified with him so that the body ruled by sin
might be done away with, that we should no longer be slaves to sin – because
anyone who has died has been set free from sin.

ROMANS 6:6–7

Corpses can't be tempted. Corpses can't sin. The gospel offers not only
forgiveness but the hope of change because the power of *self*ishness is done
away with on the Cross. When I surrender myself to Christ, I am united with
him in his death on the Cross and my sinful nature dies with him.

"Father, thank you for this amazing promise that
the old sinful patterns have no authority to rule my life!"

THE GIFT OF THE CROSS

Don't let's confuse 'dying to self' with twisted self-hatred. Becoming Christlike makes us *more* like ourselves. God's plan is not to eradicate us but *in order that ... we may live a new life* (Romans 6:4) the life you were originally designed for. God won't stamp out your individuality; he created it. God likes you.

The Cross sets us free to be who we were created to be. It is the nail-pierced hands of Jesus that offer us all the blessings promised to God's people. For centuries, church leaders have made the sign of the Cross as a sign of blessing because every blessing comes through the Cross.

When I survey the wondrous cross
On which the Prince of glory died,
My richest gain I count but loss,
And pour contempt on all my pride.
ISAAC WATTS

LIVING THE NEW LIFE

The glory of our story is that it doesn't finish in the grave. If you entrust your life to Jesus, you not only die with Christ – you are raised to new life with him. You are united with the one who overcame every temptation (Romans 6:5). That means that no sin pattern has authority to rule you. Our part is to *daily* take on the yoke of this teaching;

count yourselves dead to sin
but alive to God in Christ Jesus.
ROMANS 6:11

The question is, 'Will I live in this new reality? Will I take on this yoke?' As Terry Virgo explains, it's like changing your watch when you change time zone. It's more than the power of positive thinking, it's adjusting to the new reality.

 "Jesus thank you for the wonderful truth that I am dead to sin and alive to you!"

A yoke of grace

Sin shall no longer be your master, because you are not under the law,
but under grace.
ROMANS 6:14

Thérèse of Lisieux describes the Christian life as lots of little deaths. We can daily choose to draw on the power of the Cross and put selfishness to death. It is like living in an old house which has been rewired. Every day we can either plug into the old faulty wiring or plug into the new wiring. God is constantly calling us to plug into what he has done for us in Christ. We are not to be occupied with our sin but rather with our Saviour.

This teaching is a million miles from the heavy yoke that the Pharisees laid on the people. That's why taking on your Cross is taking on a yoke inscribed with the word 'Grace'.

 How would it change your week if you trusted
that God offers grace for every moment of every day?

ALIVE TO GOD

Count yourselves dead to sin
but alive to God in Christ Jesus.
ROMANS 6:11

We not only die to sin – we live *to God*. We are offered not only a yoke of teaching but a living relationship with the best, most gentle, patient and committed teacher ever. Jesus says,

'No one knows the Son the way the Father does, nor the Father the way the Son does. But I'm not keeping it to myself; I'm ready to go over it line by line with anyone willing to listen.'
MATTHEW 11:27 MSG

As we keep company with Christ, we become like him.

'Walk with me and work with me – watch how I do it. Learn the unforced rhythms of grace. I won't lay anything heavy or ill-fitting on you. Keep company with me and you'll learn to live freely and lightly.'
MATTHEW 11:27–30 MSG

What can I do to keep company with the Lord today?

A new name

It is for freedom that Christ has set us free. Stand firm, then,
and do not let yourselves be burdened again
by a yoke of slavery.
GALATIANS 5:1

Today God invites me to come under his yoke.

As we daily come under the grace yoke, he sets us free.

As we daily lay down our lives before him,
he hands them back made new.

And day by day, the Holy Spirit, the finger of God,
writes his wonderful name on our lives.

 "Lord, may you write your name on my heart just
as you wrote your law on those tablets of stone."

It is for freedom that Christ has
set us free. Stand firm, then,
and do not let yourselves be burdened again
by a yoke of slavery.

Galatians 5:1

Blessed in the Beloved

"'The LORD bless you and keep you,
The LORD make his face shine on you and be gracious to you;
The LORD turn his face towards you and give you peace.'"
'So they will put my name on the Israelites, and I will bless them.'

NUMBERS 6:24–27

OVERFLOWING ABOUNDING LOVE

The Father, the Son and the Holy Spirit are an eternally perfect and satisfied community of love. So why create you? God had no need of you. It was simply that God wanted to welcome us into that community of love. In a world where rejection is commonplace, we need to know that the Father, the Son and the Holy Spirit are not a closed circle of friendship but an open one.

This is the God whom Augustine addresses in his Confessions,

You gather all things to yourself, though you suffer no need. You support, you fill, and you protect all things. You create them, nourish them, and bring them to perfection. You seek to make them your own, though you lack for nothing.

It is simply because God loves us that he wants to bless us. He has no secret agenda, nothing to gain because he lacks nothing. In himself, he is all in all, and his desire to bless us is an overflow of the abundance of his love.

 Praise God who abounds in steadfast love.
(Psalm 103:8)

THE GIFT OF THE LOVE OF THE TRINITY

God created us so that the joy He has in Himself might be ours. God doesn't simply think about Himself or talk to Himself. He enjoys Himself! He celebrates with infinite and eternal intensity the beauty of who He is as Father, Son, and Holy Spirit. And we've been created to join the party![24]

SAM STORMS

Listen to Jesus,

'As the Father has loved me, so have I loved you.'
JOHN 15:9

Extraordinary! We are offered the same quality of love from Jesus that exists within the Trinity. Jesus loves us as much as the Father loves him – that is love greater than any love we have ever experienced. As if that was not enough, Jesus tells us that the Father too loves us as much as he loves the Son (John 17:23). There is no hierarchy of love, no favourites.

Can you begin to take this in?
The Father loves you as much as he
loves his beloved Son.

BE LOVED

See what great love that the Father has lavished on us,
that we should be called children of God!

1 JOHN 3:1

Asked what matters most, Jesus replied that it is to love the Lord with all you are and love your neighbour as yourself (Mark 12:30-31). But how can we possibly love as Jesus asks? It all comes back to his love –

We love because he first loved us.

1 JOHN 4:19

Our loving depends on us drawing on his endless love for us. When we live as the beloved, we love.

Being loved is wonderful; being the beloved is even better because it is a permanent status. God first loved you, he loves you now and he always will.

You are the beloved so be loved.
As you welcome him, God will pour his
love into your heart by his Holy Spirit.

Thank you that I am lavishly loved today!

Favoured

Deep down, many of us believe that God prefers other people to us –
that he has favourites. Not true!

The Greek word for 'favour' is only used a couple of times in the New Testament.
An angel comes to Mary when she is chosen to bear Christ saying, 'Greetings, you
who are highly favoured!' (Luke 1:28). Wonderfully, Paul chooses this same word
in his letter to the Ephesians when he speaks of God's grace, with which he has
'favored us with in the Beloved' (Ephesians 1:6 Holman).

What holds us back from receiving this great truth? Is it memories of past
rejections, the party invitations you never received, the people who let you
down? Trust God today that you are favoured in the Beloved.

"My loving Father, I am so sorry for when
I have lived in the lie that you would turn me away.
May my life be lived in the praise of your glorious grace,
with which you have favoured me in the Beloved."

INVITED TO THE PARTY

God's attitude to us is the opposite of rejection; he personally invites us to the greatest party ever given. Yet too often we act like the older brother in Jesus' story of the two sons, refusing to join the party. The father begs his older son to come in but the story ends without resolution. It leaves the question open, 'Will we join the celebration?'

'The older brother […] refused to go in. So his father went out and pleaded with him […] "My son," the father said, "you are always with me, and everything I have is yours."'

LUKE 15:28, 31

In that culture, it would have been a shocking loss of dignity for a father to plead with his son. Our God was willing to lay down the dignity and power of heaven to make himself as small and vulnerable as a baby – to plead with us to join the eternal party. How will we respond? Will we resist our Father's favour? Will we see ourselves as slaves or sons?

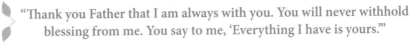

"Thank you Father that I am always with you. You will never withhold blessing from me. You say to me, 'Everything I have is yours.'"

Blessed to be a blessing

When we claim and constantly reclaim the truth of being the chosen ones, we soon discover within ourselves a deep desire to reveal to others their own chosenness.
HENRI NOUWEN

When we deliberately take our place in the Beloved, petty jealousies release their grip and the wall of selfishness that constricts our hearts begins to crumble. We begin to see that we have more than enough to share.

God delights to reveal his love to us through each other,
Christ plays in ten thousand places,
Lovely in limbs, lovely in eyes not his,
To the Father, through the features of men's faces.
GERARD MANLEY HOPKINS, *AS KINGFISHERS CATCH FIRE*

Like Abraham, we are blessed to become a blessing to others. That's how it works.

 Ask your heavenly Father to show you
how he has made you to be a blessing to others.

THE WIDENING CIRCLE

If we see Him alone, we do not see him at all. If we see Him, we see with and round Him in ever-widening circles, His disciples, the people, His enemies and the countless millions who have not yet heard His name.

KARL BARTH

We don't ask God to bless us just for ourselves but always with a view to this widening circle. With the Psalmist, we pray,

May God be gracious to us and bless us
and make his face shine upon us –
so that your ways may be known on earth,
your salvation among all nations.

PSALM 67:1–2

Could you draw some of the circles in your life where you are asking God for his blessing? You could pray this verse over each circle – beginning with your family and friends and widening out to your workplace and your street right out to your nation and to the world.

GOD'S SURPRISING STRATEGY

God has given to his church the great privilege of blessing others. He chose to speak the blessing of Numbers 6 through his priests. Now he makes us a royal priesthood (1 Peter 2:9), a channel of his blessing to others.

You don't have to be a church minister; if you are in Christ, every spiritual blessing is yours and you are empowered to bless others. You don't have to be perfect; after all, God chose flawed Aaron to be the first one to speak his great blessing over his people. Who could you speak blessing over today? Who could you build up? God's words of blessing have great power and he is calling us to speak them.

Make a list of the people that God has put on your heart and choose different lines from the blessing from Numbers 6 to pray over them, according to their need and how God guides you.

GIVE IT AWAY

'Give and it will be given to you ... pressed down,
shaken together and running over ...'
LUKE 6:38

Jesus told us that the measure we use will be measured to us. Open your hands to give and they will be filled with blessing. Stay tight-fisted and you end up clutching nothing. This is true for individuals and for churches. The church that lapses from the calling to bless, stagnates like water with nowhere to go. Giving multiplies blessing.

In the words of Jim Elliott, who was martyred by Auca Indians, 'He is no fool who gives what he cannot keep to gain that which he cannot lose.' The blessing we receive is better than a plump bank balance or lofty status. We encounter the heart of God.

It is a gift of God to us to be able to share our love with others.
MOTHER TERESA (NOBEL PEACE PRIZE SPEECH)

"Thank you Father for the gift of giving,
a gift blessed above all others."

Abundantly Blessed

God is able to bless you abundantly,
so that in all things at all times,
having all that you need,
you will abound in every good work.
2 CORINTHIANS 9:8

The God of abounding love made us in his image to abound in love and good works. Praise God that we don't do good works to earn his favour but because we already have it.

What a wonderful God we have – inordinately generous and lavishly loving … intent on blessing us and on making us a blessing!

What blessing could you give away today?
Is there someone you can introduce to Jesus?
Are there prayers of blessing that he wants you to pray?
Is there a gift to be given, a text to send,
a letter to write, a visit to be made?

BLESSED IN THE BELOVED

Praise be to the God and Father of our Lord Jesus Christ, who has blessed us in the heavenly realms with every spiritual blessing in Christ!

EPHESIANS 1:3

How blessed is God! And what a blessing he is! He's the Father of our Master, Jesus Christ, and takes us to the high places of blessing in him. Long before he laid down earth's foundations, he had us in mind, had settled on us as the focus of his love, to be made whole and holy by his love. Long, long ago he decided to adopt us into his family through Jesus Christ. (What pleasure he took in planning this!) He wanted us to enter into the celebration of his lavish gift-giving by the hand of his beloved Son.

*Because of the sacrifice of the Messiah, his blood poured out on the altar of the Cross, we're a free people free of penalties and punishments chalked up by all our misdeeds. And not just barely free, either. **Abundantly** free! He thought of everything, provided for everything we could possibly need, letting us in on the plans he took such delight in making. He set it all out before us in Christ, a long-range plan in which everything would be brought together and summed up in him, everything in deepest heaven, everything on planet earth.*

It's in Christ that we find out who we are and what we are living for.

EPHESIANS 1:3–11 MSG

 Make a list of all the blessings mentioned in these verses. Then read it aloud first putting your name in wherever Paul writes 'us' and then finally by putting 'me' where Paul writes 'us'.

NOTES

1 John Piper, 'How Can I Hope? New birth!'. http://www.desiringgod.org/sermons/how-can-i-hope-new-birth .

2 Brother Lawrence, *The Practice of the Presence of God*, translated by E.M. Blaiklock (Hodder & Stoughton, 1988).

3 *A Diary of Private Prayer* by John Baillie, edited by Susannah Wright (Simon & Schuster, 2014).

4 John Donne wrote a beautiful sonnet with the line, 'Immensity cloistered in thy dear womb' which inspired this poem.

5 C. S. Lewis, *The Screwtape Letters*, (Harper Collins, 2002) p. 17.

6 From Bach, *Cantata* BWV 147 .

7 *Andrew Murray On Prayer* (Whitaker House, 1998).

8 Dallas Willard helpfully outlines these disciplines in his book, *The Spirit of the Disciplines* (HarperOne, 1999).

9 Eric Metaxas, *Bonhoeffer: Pastor, Martyr, Prophet, Spy* (Thomas Nelson, 2010).

10 Dietrich Bonhoeffer, *Life Together and Prayerbook of the Bible* (vol. 5 of Dietrich Bonhoeffer Works; Minneapolis: Fortress Press, 1996).

11 Romans 4:22.

12 Terry Virgo, *God's Lavish Grace*, (Monarch, 2004).

13 Thirteenth-century prayer written by Richard, Bishop of Chichester.

14 Lewis B. Smedes, *Forgive and Forget: Healing the Hurts We Don't Deserve* (HarperSanFrancisco, 2007).

15 Desmond Tutu, *No Future Without Forgiveness*, (Rider, 2000).

16 Cornelius Plantinga,Jr, *Not the Way It's Supposed to Be: A Breviary of Sin* (Eerdmans, 1995).

17 Frederick Dale Bruner *Matthew; A Commentary: The Churchbook, Matthew 13-28* (Eerdmans, 2004).

18 Cindy Wooden, 'Conflict between Christians makes Christ's body suffer, says Pope' *Catholic Herald*, 19 June 2013. http://www.catholicherald.co.uk/news/2013/06/19/conflicts-makes-christs-body-suffer-says-pope/ .

19 John Piper, *Desiring God: Meditations of a Christian Hedonist* (IVP, 2004).

20 Deuteronomy 16:11; 1 Chronicles 16:10; Psalm 32:11; Philippians 4:4 to name but a few.

21 Dr Lucy Peppiatt, *The Disciple* (Wipf & Stock 2012).

22 C. S. Lewis, *Mere Christianity* (HarperOne reprinted 2012).

23 John Stott, *The Radical Disciple* (IVP, 2010).

24 Sam Storms, 'A Christian Theory of Everything', March 21, 2006. http://www.samstorms.com/enjoying-god-blog/post/a-christian-theory-of-everything .

Levels
3-4

Level Up

MATHS

Author team: Ian Boote
Caroline Clissold
John Davis
Bobbie Johns
Robert Ward-Penny
Jeanette Whiteman

LiveText

Heinemann

Heinemann is an imprint of Pearson Education Limited, a company incorporated in England and Wales, having its registered office at Edinburgh Gate, Harlow, Essex, CM20 2JE. Registered company number: 872828

www.heinemann.co.uk

Heinemann is a registered trademark of Pearson Education Limited

Text © Pearson Education Limited, 2009

First published 2009

13 12
10 9 8 7 6 5 4 3

British Library Cataloguing in Publication Data is available from the British Library on request.

ISBN 978 0 435537 44 9

Editorial consultancy by Jean Carnall
Editorial development by Project One Publishing Solutions, Scotland
Designed and typeset by Artistix
Illustrated by Beehive
Cover design by Tom Cole (Seamonster Design)
Cover photo/illustration © Pearson Education Limited
Printed in China (SWTC/03)

Contents

Welcome to Level Up Maths!

Level Up Maths is an inspirational new course for today's classroom. With stunning textbooks and amazing software, Key Stage 3 Maths has simply never looked this good!

Workbook pages

This workbook is divided into 16 units. For each workbook page there is a full lesson plan in the Planning and Assessment Pack. There are also three revision sections (one per term) which give you the opportunity to check your understanding. Each section has a quick quiz, check up questions and an extended activity.

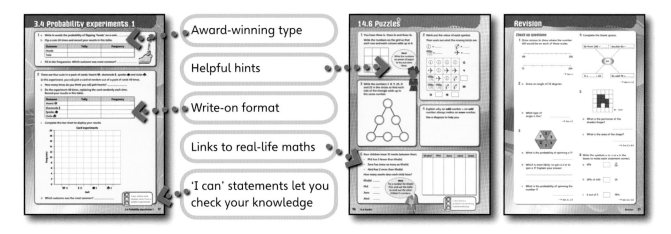

- Award-winning type
- Helpful hints
- Write-on format
- Links to real-life maths
- 'I can' statements let you check your knowledge

Links to Level Up Maths Levels 5–7

These features from the Level Up Maths Levels 5–7 textbook and LiveText CD-ROM are designed for pupils working on the Levels 3–4 workbook. The Levels 3–4 Planning and Assessment Pack shows how.

Levels 5–7 Textbook
Unit introduction

Each unit begins with an introduction. These include a striking background image to set the scene and short activities.

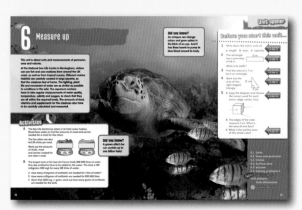

Special activities highlight some intriguing **applications and implications of maths**. Where in history and culture does today's maths come from? How does it affect our lives? Why is it so important to get it right?

LiveText software

The LiveText software for Level Up Maths Levels 3–5 also gives you a wide range of additional interactive explanations, games, activities and extra questions. Simply turn the pages of the electronic book and explore!

LiveText

Glossary – contains definitions of key terms. Play audio to hear translations in Bengali, Gujarati, Punjabi, Turkish and Urdu.

Resources – a comprehensive list of all relevant resources plus lesson plans.

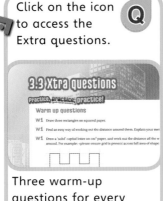

Click on the icon to access the Extra questions.

Three warm-up questions for every page give a gentle lead-in to the Level 3–5 questions on the page.

Competitive maths games

You may need a partner.

Interactive

Interactive

We've scoured the planet to find examples of the World's greatest maths for you to try. You may find yourself planning a rock concert or designing the ultimate paper plane.

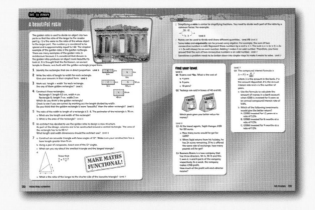

Unit plenary

Each unit ends with an extended activity to help you practise functional maths and demonstrate your understanding. There are also levelled check up questions to try.

1.1 All in the head

1 Put the balls in the holes so that each line adds up to the target number.

a

 2 **3**

 4 **5**

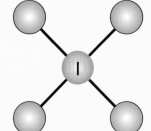

TARGET: 8

b

 30 **40**

 50 **60**

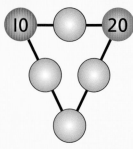

TARGET: 90

2 Work out the answers to these additions and subtractions in your head.

a 62 + 13 = _75_

   74 + 12 = _____

   54 + 21 = _____

   28 + 33 = _____

   67 + 14 = _____

   65 + 29 = _____

   36 + 87 = _____

> 62 add 10 is 72, now add the extra 3 to make 75.

b 87 – 24 = _63_

   67 – 12 = _____

   74 – 23 = _____

   54 – 31 = _____

   81 – 33 = _____

   68 – 19 = _____

   94 – 28 = _____

> 87 take away 20 is 67, now take away the extra 4 to make 63.

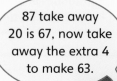

3 Every prize on the tombola stall has a ticket with a 2-digit number on.

Write down the pair of items that:

a add up to the largest number

   _____

b have a difference of 79

   _____

c add up to a number that looks the same if it is written backwards

   _____

4 Work out the answers in your head:

  a 31 + 45 = _____   b 53 + 29 = _____   c 67 – 43 = _____

 I can add or subtract any pair of numbers less than 100.

1.2 Spot the difference

1 Draw a line between any Dalmatians that have a difference which is a **multiple of 10**.

2 a Fill in the missing numbers to work out the difference between 28 and 73.

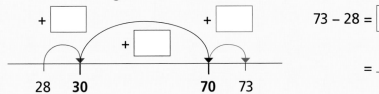

$$73 - 28 = \boxed{} + \boxed{} + \boxed{}$$

$$= \underline{}$$

Use a similar method to work out the difference between 26 and 92.

b Fill in the missing numbers to help you work out the difference between 526 and 193.

$$+\boxed{} \qquad +\boxed{}$$

$$+\boxed{}$$

193 200   500 526

$$526 - 193 = \boxed{} + \boxed{} + \boxed{}$$

$$= \underline{}$$

Use a similar method to work out the difference between 399 and 713.

3 Work out these differences in your head by counting up through **multiples of 10, 100 or 1000**.

a   85 – 48 = _____

b   63 – 18 = _____

c   61 – 29 = _____

d   745 – 298 = _____

e   820 – 195 = _____

f   937 – 580 = _____

g   6401 – 1998 = _____

h   8209 – 5500 = _____

i   9640 – 2850 = _____

4 Work out these differences in your head by counting up.

a   73 – 19 = _____

b   624 – 198 = _____

c   5028 – 1990 = _____

d   4326 – 2299 = _____

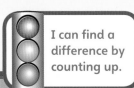

I can find a difference by counting up.

1.3 Next to nothing

1 Write the missing numbers on the thermometer.

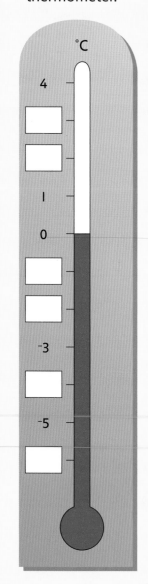

°C

4

1

0

-3

-5

2 Draw a circle around the **coldest** fridge.

-5°C

2°C

-8°C

3
a What temperature is 7° warmer than -5°C? _____

b What temperature is 8° warmer than -4°C? _____

c What number is 5 more than -3? _____

d What number is 4 more than -1? _____

e What number is 4 more than -4? _____

f What temperature is 6° less than 1°C? _____

g What temperature is 7° less than 3°C? _____

h What number is 5 less than 2? _____

i What number is 3 less than 0? _____

j What number is 2 less than -6? _____

4 Write these changes to bank accounts as number sentences. Calculate the final bank balances.

a Adam has £5 in his account and withdraws £12. _____

b Brianna has -£8 in her account and deposits £10. _____

c Cody has £3 in his account and withdraws £20. _____

5 The temperature in a town was 4°C, but it dropped by 6°C overnight. How cold was the town that night?

_____

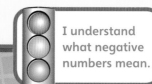

I understand what negative numbers mean.

1.4 Using negative numbers

1 Solve the code to find out where polar bears live.

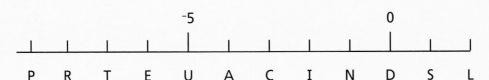

-5   0

P   R   T   E   U   A   C   I   N   D   S   L

Polar bears live at the

-4   -8   -3   -7   -2   -3   -3   -2   -8   -3   2   -6

_____

2 For each pair of shapes, circle the larger number and write down their difference.

a   The difference is __4__.

b   The difference is _____.

c   The difference is _____.

d   The difference is _____.

e   The difference is _____.

3 Use the sign change key on your calculator to work out the answers.

a   7 + ⁻2 = _____

b   6 + ⁻9 = _____

c   ⁻3 + ⁻5 = _____

d   ⁻2 + 8 = _____

e   ⁻15 − 3 = _____

f   13 − ⁻4 = _____

g   ⁻8 − ⁻8 = _____

h   ⁻42 + ⁻33 = _____

i   185 + ⁻218 = _____

The sign change key usually looks like this or this .

4 Write these numbers in order from smallest to largest:

3   -5   -2   1   -7

_____

I can put positive and negative numbers in order.

1.5 Step by step

1 Write the missing numbers on these sequence ladders.

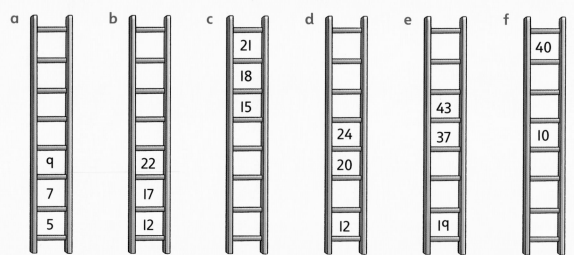

- **g** Draw a star at the top of any ladder which only has **odd numbers**.
- **h** Draw a smiley face at the top of any ladder which only has **multiples of 4**.

2 Use the rule and write the first five terms of each sequence.

- **a** Start at 16, add 3.
- **b** Start at 91, add 11.
- **c** Start at $56\frac{1}{2}$, subtract 4.
- **d** Start at 5, double.
- **e** Use the sequence and write the rule.

  Start at _____, _____.

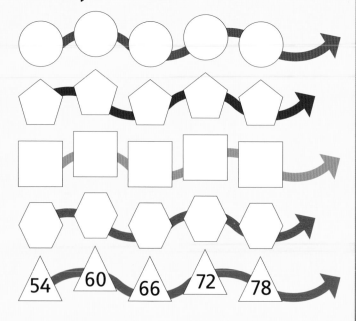

3 Write the next three numbers of each sequence.

- **a** 19, 26, 33, 40, _____, _____, _____
- **b** 41, 39, 37, 35, _____, _____, _____
- **c** 20, 15, 10, 5, _____, _____, _____
- **d** 6.2, 6.4, 6.6, 6.8, _____, _____, _____

I can find the next three numbers of a sequence.

1.6 Matching sequences

1 Match each sequence with its rule. Use the empty box to describe the sequence that is left over.

a   Even numbers

b   Start at 2, add 3

c   Multiples of 7

d   Start at 7, add 9

e

7, 16, 25, 34, …

2, 4, 6, 8, …

7, 14, 21, 28, …

2, 6, 18, 54, …

2, 5, 8, 11, …

2 Draw the next picture in each sequence. Write the number of matchsticks used under each picture. Describe the sequence.

a

Start at _____,

add _____.

☐   ☐   ☐   ☐

b

  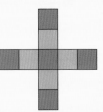

_____

_____

☐   ☐   ☐   ☐

c   What is the special name for the second sequence? _____

3 Look at this sequence. The sequence keeps growing.
How many squares would be in the 8th picture?

Hint!
Write the sequence in numbers.

4 Describe each sequence in words.

a   3, 8, 13, 18, 23, …   _____

b   56, 28, 14, 7, 3.5, …   _____

2.1 Lines

1 a Convert these measurements so that they are in millimetres.

4.5 cm _____   3 cm 4 mm _____   7.9 cm _____   36 cm 8 mm _____   13.2 cm _____

b Write the measurements in order of size, from the shortest to the longest.

_____

2 Estimate the length of each line. Then measure it.

a _____   Estimate _____   Actual _____

b _____   Estimate _____   Actual _____

c _____   Estimate _____   Actual _____

d _____   Estimate _____   Actual _____

e _____

Estimate _____   Actual _____

f _____

Estimate _____   Actual _____

How close were you?

a _____   b _____   c _____

d _____   e _____   f _____

3 Look at the diagram.

a Mark the **parallel** ⇥ and **perpendicular** ⊥ lines.

b Which lines are parallel to each other?

_____ and _____   _____ and _____

c Which lines are perpendicular to each other?

_____ and _____   _____ and _____

_____ and _____   _____ and _____

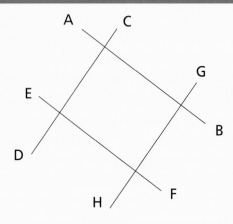

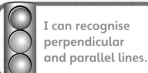

I can recognise
perpendicular
and parallel lines.

2.2 Angles

1 Label the angles inside this shape.
Use these words:

acute

right

obtuse

reflex

2 a Draw an **irregular pentagon** with at least one right angle and acute, obtuse and reflex angles.

b Label each angle with a sensible estimate of its size.

3 The sizes of these angles are: 45°, 90°, 90°, 115° and 250°. Label which is which.

a

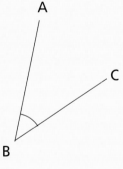

b

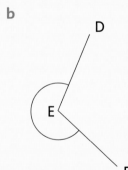

c

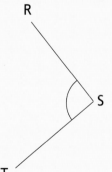

d

e

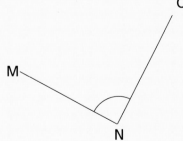

Remember!
Think about the type of angle first!

I can estimate the size of angles in degrees.

2.3 Measuring angles

1 a Peter thinks angle ABC measures 150°. He thinks angle DEF is 80°.

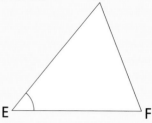

Are Peter's estimates reasonable? _____

b Use a protractor to measure the angles and find out how close he was.

∠ ABC _____   ∠ DEF _____

2 a Follow these instructions to draw a triangle.

- Draw AB and AC at right angles to each other.

- AB is 5 cm long, AC is 6 cm.

- Join B and C with a line.

b Measure angles ABC and ACB. What is their size?

∠ ABC _____   ∠ ACB _____

3 a Estimate the size of the angles at the centre of the circle. Then measure them.

b Use a calculator to work out the difference between your estimate and the actual measurement.

c Were your estimates close?

Estimate
Actual
Difference

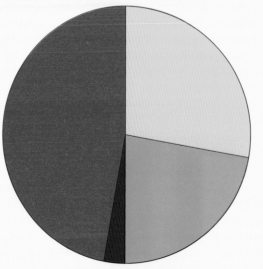

Estimate
Actual
Difference

Estimate
Actual
Difference

Estimate
Actual
Difference

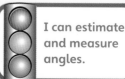

I can estimate and measure angles.

2.4 Drawing and measuring angles

1 Mark the angles shown on these protractors.

a 30°

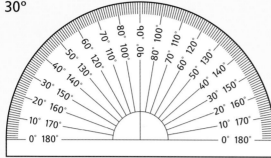

b 60°

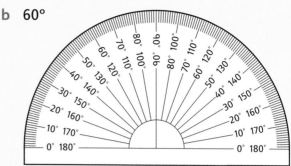

c 10°

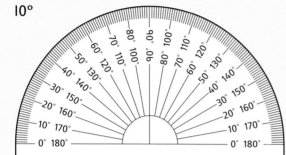

d 80°

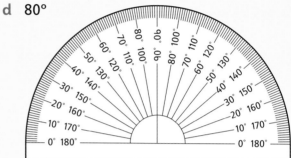

2 Construct these angles. Use the baselines given.

a 25°

b 85°

c 5°

d 75°

3 Construct angles on these lines.

a 70°

b 45°

I can construct acute angles.

2.5 Triangles

1 Draw an example of each type of triangle. Mark any equal sides and angles.

Equilateral	Isosceles	Right-angled isosceles	Scalene	Right-angled scalene

2 a What type of triangle makes this shape? _____

How do you know this? _____

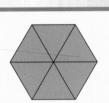

b List all the examples of each type of triangle in this equilateral triangle ABF.

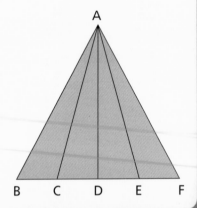

Equilateral _____

Rt-angled isosceles _____

Isosceles _____

Rt-angled scalene _____

Scalene _____

3 Describe these triangles using their properties. Delete the words that do not apply.

Triangle	Sides	Angles
Equilateral	all the same / two the same / none the same	all equal / two equal / none equal / one right angle
Isosceles	all the same / two the same / none the same	all equal / two equal / none equal / one right angle
Right-angled isosceles	all the same / two the same / none the same	all equal / two equal / none equal / one right angle
Scalene	all the same / two the same / none the same	all equal / two equal / none equal / one right angle
Right-angled scalene	all the same / two the same / none the same	all equal / two equal / none equal / one right angle

I can identify triangles from their descriptions.

2.6 Quadrilaterals

1 a Write the name of each quadrilateral.

A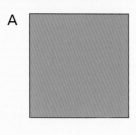

B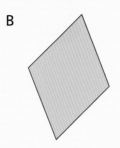

C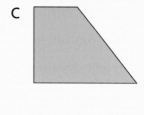

_____

_____

_____

D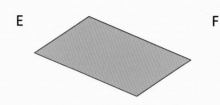

E

F

_____

_____

_____

b Which of these shapes are parallelograms? _____

2 Take each of the shapes from question I, one at a time. Follow this diagram and write the name of the shape at the end of a 'branch'.

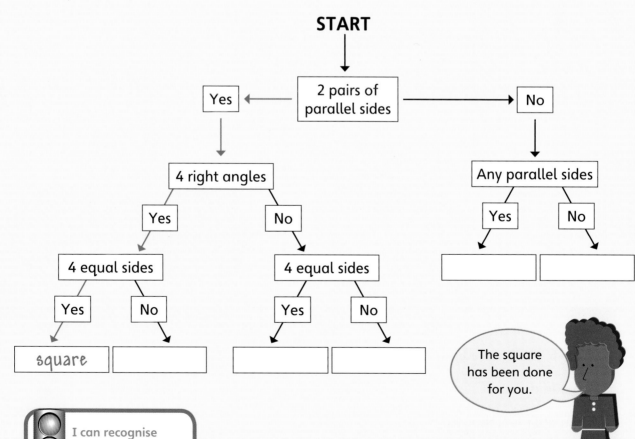

The square has been done for you.

I can recognise and name common quadrilaterals.

3.1 Introducing probability

1 Match the events with words that describe their probability of happening.

   a   It will rain tomorrow.

   b   A flipped coin will land on heads.

   c   The Sun will rise tomorrow.

   d   A cow will jump over the Moon.

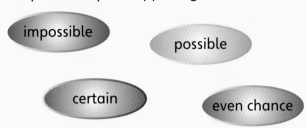

impossible   possible   certain   even chance

2 Make up an event to match the given probability.

likely

impossible

unlikely

3 Choose words from questions 1 and 2 to describe the probability of each outcome when these spinners are spun once.

Colour	Spinner A	Spinner B
Blue	even chance	
Red		
Yellow		

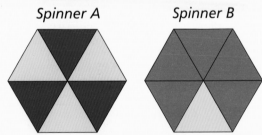

Spinner A   Spinner B

4 A fair 1–6 dice is rolled once. Describe in words the probability of rolling:

   a   an odd number   _____

   b   a number less than 10   _____

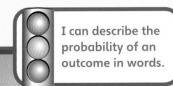

I can describe the probability of an outcome in words.

3.2 The probability scale

1 You can mark the probability of an event happening on a probability scale.
   A probability scale goes between 0 and I.

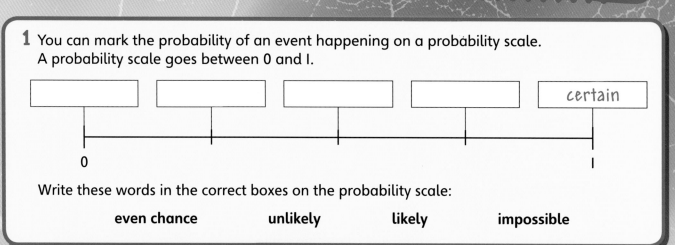

| | | | | certain |

0   I

Write these words in the correct boxes on the probability scale:

even chance   **unlikely**   **likely**   **impossible**

2 Kathy picks a card from a **full pack** of cards. Match each event to its letter on this
   probability scale.

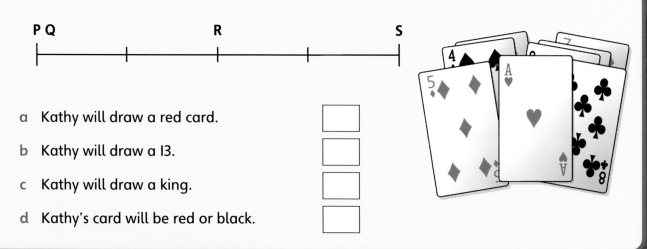

P Q   R   S

a   Kathy will draw a red card.

b   Kathy will draw a I3.

c   Kathy will draw a king.

d   Kathy's card will be red or black.

3 a   An event is **impossible**.
       Write down its probability as a number.   _____

   b   Another event is **certain**.
       Write down its probability as a number.   _____

   c   A third event has a probability of $\frac{1}{2}$.
       Describe its probability in words.   _____

Hint!
Use the probability
scale in question I
to help.

4 Mark events X, Y and Z in the correct places on this probability scale.

0   I

X: The day after Monday will be Tuesday.

Y: You will get 'heads' if you flip a fair coin.

Z: You will win the National Lottery.

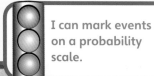

I can mark events
on a probability
scale.

3.3 What are the chances?

1 Pete plays a game with three spinners.

A    B 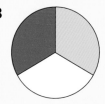   C

Write whether each statement is true or false.

a   Pete is unlikely to get yellow with spinner A.   _____

b   Spinner B has the highest probability of getting white.   _____

c   Spinner C has an even chance of getting blue.   _____

d   The probability of getting red on spinner A is 0.   _____

e   Spinner C is more likely to land on white than spinner A.   _____

2 A bag contains five balls. One is red, one is yellow and the others are white. Alex picks a ball from the bag at random. Write the probability of picking each colour as a number.

a   a red ball   _____

b   a purple ball   _____

c   a white ball   _____

3 A box of chocolates contains ten chocolates. Two are caramels, three are toffees and five contain nuts. Robin closes her eyes and picks a chocolate.

a   Which type of chocolate is least likely to be picked?   _____

b   Which type of chocolate has an even chance of being picked?   _____

c   Write the probability of picking a toffee as a fraction.   _____

4 A teacher has the four number cards shown. She shuffles them and picks one at random. Write down the probability of each event.

a   She picks a red card.   _____   **2** **3** **5** **7**

b   She picks a 7.   _____

c   She picks an even number.   _____

d   She picks a card that is red **and** even.   _____

 I can find probabilities of simple events.

3.4 Probability experiments 1

1 a Write in words the probability of flipping 'heads' on a coin. _____

   b Flip a coin 20 times and record your results in this table.

Outcome	Tally	Frequency
Heads		
Tails		

   c Fill in the frequencies. Which outcome was more common? _____

2 There are four suits in a pack of cards: hearts ♥, diamonds ♦, spades ♠ and clubs ♣.

   In this experiment, you will pick a card at random out of a pack of cards 40 times.

   a How many times do you think you will pick hearts? _____

   b Do the experiment 40 times, replacing the card randomly each time.
      Record your results in this table.

Outcome	Tally	Frequency
Hearts ♥		
Diamonds ♦		
Spades ♠		
Clubs ♣		

   c Complete this bar chart to display your results.

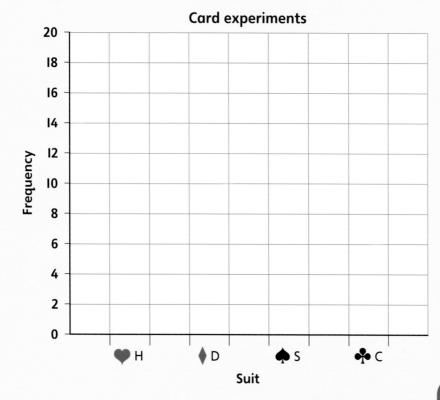

   Card experiments

   d Which outcome was the most common? _____

I can collect and display data from a simple experiment.

3.5 Probability experiments 2

1 In this experiment you will roll three dice and add their scores together.

   a What is the largest total you could get? _____

   b What is the smallest total you could get? _____

   c What is the probability of rolling a total of 2 with three dice? _____

   d Which number or numbers do you think will come up the most often? Write your prediction. _____

Do the experiment and record your results in the table.

Total	Tally	Frequency
3		
4		
5		
6		
7		
8		
9		
10		
11		
12		
13		
14		
15		
16		
17		
18		

e Which totals occurred most frequently?

_____

f Which totals occurred least frequently?

_____

g Explain this finding.

_____

_____

_____

_____

h Was your prediction right?

_____

   i Use this grid to draw a bar chart to display your results.

   j Compare your results with a partner's results. Were they similar?

_____

I can investigate a problem using maths.

3.6 Interpreting experiments

1 Ben asks people which activity they do most at the sports centre. His results are shown in this table.

Activity	Tally	Frequency
Swimming pool	JHT JHT II	
Gym	JHT JHT JHT JHT JHT III	
Squash courts	JHT II	
Other	III	

a Fill in the frequencies.

b How many people did Ben ask altogether? _____

c Ben asks the next person who comes in what they are going to do. What is their answer most likely to be? _____

2 In a scientific experiment, a reaction can produce three types of particle: delta, gamma or omega. The bar chart shows the results of the experiment.

a How many reactions produced omega particles? _____

b Which particle type was least likely? _____

c What is the probability of a reaction producing a gamma particle:

- in words _____

- as a number _____

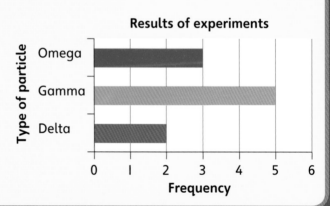

Results of experiments

3 Sue finds out people's favourite type of pizza. She asks 15 people in Year 7 and 15 people in Year 9. Her results are shown here.

Year 7

Pizza	Frequency
Plain	4
Hawaiian	8
BBQ	2
Vegetarian	1

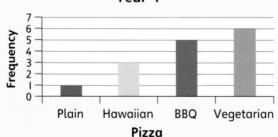

Year 9

a Which flavour was most common in Year 9? _____

b How many people in Year 9 liked Hawaiian best? _____

c How many more people in Year 9 said BBQ than in Year 7? _____

d If a person said they liked Hawaiian best, which Year group were they more likely to be in? _____

I can read data from bar charts and frequency tables.

4.1 Place to place

1 Rick has these three cards. He can make different numbers by putting them in different orders.

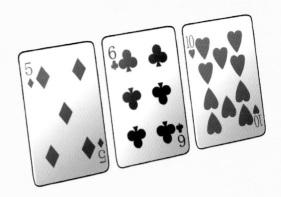

   a What is the largest number Rick can make? Write this number in digits and words.

      _____

   b What is the smallest number Rick can make? Write this number in digits and words.

      _____

2 Write the amounts in figures.

   a Thirty-seven point eight two   _____

   b One hundred and sixteen point four   _____

   c Five thousand, two hundred and nine   _____

3 Write the answers.

   a 93×10 = _____   b 23×100 = _____

   c 780×100 = _____   d 567×1000 = _____

   e $490 \div 10$ = _____   f $7600 \div 100$ = _____

   g 81×10 = _____   h $58000 \div 1000$ = _____

   i $5080 \div 10$ = _____   j 33×10 = _____

   k $29 \div 10$ = _____   l 483×100 = _____

   m 66×100 = _____   n $4672 \div 100$ = _____

   o 12×1000 = _____   p $8090 \div 1000$ = _____

4 a There are 100 centimetres in 1 metre.

     How many centimetres are there in 46 metres? _____

   b A pack of 10 pairs of socks costs £45.

     How much does one pair cost? _____

I can multiply and divide whole numbers by 10, 100 and 1000.

4.2 Sign of the times

1 Turn the egg into a chicken by finding the correct path through the maze. Double the egg number to move towards the chicken, or halve the chicken number to move back towards the egg.

7	12	24	48	102
14	28	56	116	204
18	48	112	224	448
36	106	212	416	896

2 In this times table, each symbol represents a different digit.

a Which times table is it? ________

✎ × ★ = ★

✋ × ★ = ✎ ⊙

❖ × ★ = ✎ ★

⚐ × ★ = ✋ ⊙

★ × ★ = ✋ ★

☺ × ★ = ❖ ⊙

b Use the code and complete the next line of the times table.

➘ × ★ = ____________

3 Work out the answers in your head.

a 3 × 4 = ______ b 5 × 7 = ______ c 6 × 9 = ______

d 8 × 8 = ______ e 5 × 9 = ______ f 7 × 6 = ______

g 10 × 4 = ______ h 0 × 4 = ______ i 7 × 7 = ______

j 9 × 0 = ______ k 9 × 9 = ______ l 2 × 3 × 5 = ______

m 9 × 2 × 10 = ______ n 4 × 5 × 6 = ______ o 8 × 7 × 2 = ______

4 Work out these multiplications. Use your answers to help you write down the related division facts.

a 4 × 9 = ______, so:

______ ÷ 9 = 4 and ______ ÷ 4 = 9.

b 8 × 6 = ______, so:

______ ÷ 8 = ______ and ______ ÷ 6 = ______

5 a Alan gets £7 pocket money every week. He saves for 4 weeks.

How much money will he have?

____

b Cheryl has 8 boxes of eggs. There are 6 eggs in each box.

How many eggs does she have altogether?

____

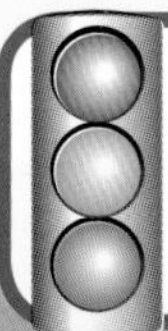

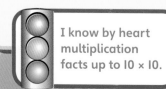

I know by heart multiplication facts up to 10 × 10.

4.3 Finding fractions

1 Shade in the correct fraction of each shape. Then fill the gaps in the table. The first shape has been shaded in for you.

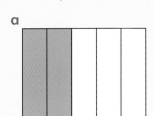
a

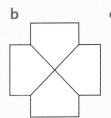
b

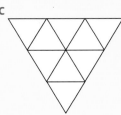
c

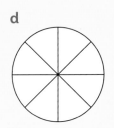
d

Shaded	$\frac{2}{5}$	$\frac{3}{4}$	$\frac{2}{9}$	$\frac{5}{8}$
Unshaded				

2 Work out these fractions and shade the answers with the correct colour to reveal the picture.

Black

$\frac{1}{5}$ of 10 $\frac{1}{2}$ of 32 $\frac{1}{8}$ of 88

$\frac{1}{3}$ of 15 $\frac{1}{2}$ of 56 $\frac{1}{2}$ of 42

Green

$\frac{1}{10}$ of 90 $\frac{1}{4}$ of 60 $\frac{1}{8}$ of 24

$\frac{1}{7}$ of 70 $\frac{1}{5}$ of 100 $\frac{1}{2}$ of 46

$\frac{1}{10}$ of 290 $\frac{1}{6}$ of 36 $\frac{1}{5}$ of 135

Blue

$\frac{1}{2}$ of 28 $\frac{1}{9}$ of 72 $\frac{1}{10}$ of 170

$\frac{1}{3}$ of 66 $\frac{1}{7}$ of 28 $\frac{1}{4}$ of 48

$\frac{1}{100}$ of 1300

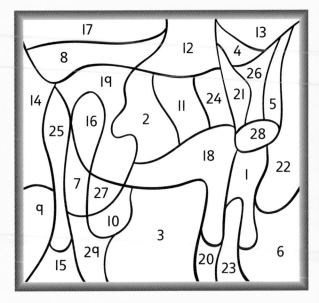

3 Complete the fraction equations.

a $\frac{1}{10}$ of 90 = ☐   b $\frac{1}{8}$ of 24 = ☐

c $\frac{1}{7}$ of 35 = ☐   d ☐ of 60 = 20

I can find simple fractions of numbers.

4.4 Equivalent fractions

1 Shade the given fraction of each shape. Show whether the first fraction is **greater than**, **less than** or **equal to** the second fraction.

a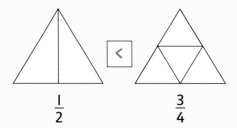

$\dfrac{1}{2}$ < $\dfrac{3}{4}$

b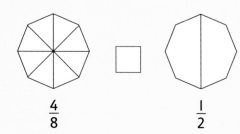

$\dfrac{4}{8}$ □ $\dfrac{1}{2}$

c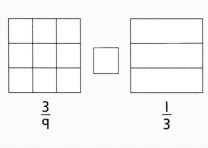

$\dfrac{3}{9}$ $\dfrac{1}{3}$

d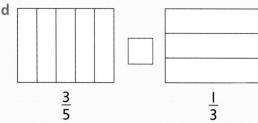

$\dfrac{3}{5}$ $\dfrac{1}{3}$

2 Fill in the boxes to make **equivalent fractions**.

a $\dfrac{1}{3} = \dfrac{\Box}{6}$

b $\dfrac{1}{5} = \dfrac{2}{\Box}$

c $\dfrac{6}{8} = \dfrac{3}{\Box}$

d $\dfrac{9}{10} = \dfrac{\Box}{100}$

e $\dfrac{4}{7} = \dfrac{\Box}{21}$

3 Write the value of the diagrams in each part as **mixed numbers** and **improper fractions**.

a

_____

b

_____

Change these improper fractions into mixed numbers.

c $\dfrac{4}{3} = $ _____

d $\dfrac{3}{2} = $ _____

e $\dfrac{11}{9} = $ _____

f $\dfrac{6}{4} = $ _____

4 Cross out the four pairs of equivalent fractions in the grid. Which fraction is left over?

$\dfrac{3}{10}$	$\dfrac{6}{16}$	$\dfrac{7}{14}$
$\dfrac{4}{5}$	$\dfrac{30}{100}$	$\dfrac{1}{2}$
$\dfrac{6}{10}$	$\dfrac{3}{8}$	$\dfrac{8}{10}$

I can identify equivalent fractions.

4.5 Point of order

1 a Use your knowledge of tenths and hundredths to fill the missing fractions and decimals.

b What is the value of the '2' in 0.28?

_____

Fraction	$\frac{4}{10}$		$\frac{7}{100}$	$\frac{37}{100}$		
Decimal		0.9			0.06	0.28

---

2 Rearrange these cards to make:

a a number between 8.6 and 8.9 _____

b a number between 5.7 and 5.8 _____

3   5   7
  8   .

---

3 Write <, > or = between each pair of decimal numbers to make the statements correct.

a   2.7   ☐   2.8

b   7.53   ☐   7.35

c   3.368   ☐   3.37

d   10.72   ☐   10.69

e   ⁻7.6   ☐   ⁻6.7

---

4 The five quickest times for the men's steeplechase are given below. Write the place (1st, 2nd, 3rd...) next to the times.

a 7:55.28 _____

b 7:59.18 _____

c 7:53.63 _____

d 7:59.08 _____

e 7:55.72 _____

---

5 Xie Qiuping of China has the longest hair in the world. It is 5.627 m.

Five boys in class 9Q measured their hair.

Adam: 7.4 cm   George: 6.9 cm   Jacob: 6.8 cm   Liam: 10.4 cm   Oliver: 7.8 cm

a Write these lengths in order, starting with the shortest.

_____

b Are these boys close to the world record? _____

---

6 Farmer Blyth wrote down the weights of eight newborn pigs. Rewrite the weights in order, starting with the lightest pig.

1.4 kg   1.45 kg   1.8 kg   1.38 kg   1.72 kg   1.5 kg   1.66 kg   1.75 kg

_____

I can write a list of decimals in order.

4.6 Percentages

1 This grid is made up of 100 squares.

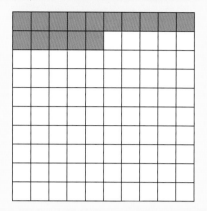

  a What percentage is coloured blue? _____

  b Colour 27% red and 41% yellow.

  c What percentage is left white? _____

2 In a survey, 25% of men admitted talking to their cars.

What percentage of men did **not** talk to their cars? _____

What percentage of cars talked back?!

3 Complete this table of equivalent fractions, decimals and percentages.

	Fraction	Decimal	Percentage
a	$\frac{73}{100}$		
b		0.62	
c			44%
d	$\frac{1}{4}$		
e			10%
f	$\frac{9}{100}$		

4 Find 10% of each amount. Then use it to find another percentage.

  a 10% of 50 is _____

     so 20% of 50 is _____

  b 10% of 750 m is _____

     so 20% of 750 m is _____

  c 10% of 60 kg is _____

     so 30% of 60 kg is _____

  d 10% of £200 is _____

     so 70% of £200 is _____

  e 10% of £50 is _____

     so 5% of £50 is _____

  f 10% of 40 cm is _____

     so 5% of 40 cm is _____

     and 15% of 40 cm is _____

5 Work out these percentages.

  a 10% of 870 g

  b 80% of £110

  c 25% of 400 ml

  d 15% of 80 m

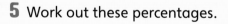

I can find 10% and other related percentages.

Remember the **magic 10%**. You can use it to find other percentages.

5.1 Relationships between operations

1 Use the number facts in the oval to work out the missing numbers in the calculations.

a 76 + 77 = ☐   b 131 − 9 = ☐   c 28 + 67 = ☐

d 122 − 65 = ☐   e 46 + 32 = ☐   f ☐ − 98 = 56

65 + 57 = 122   153 − 76 = 77

122 + 9 = 131   98 + 56 = 154   78 − 32 = 46

95 − 28 = 67

2 Write four different multiplication and division calculations using each group of numbers.

a

10 × 5 = 50

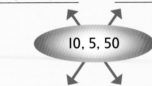
10, 5, 50

b

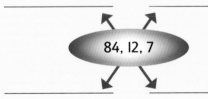
84, 12, 7

c

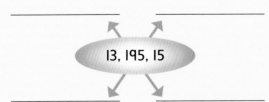
13, 195, 15

d

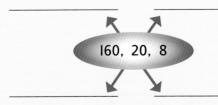
160, 20, 8

3 Write a number sentence for each problem, then use a calculator to work out the answer.

a Increase 472 by 339.

b Find the difference between 694 and 287.

c What is the product of 235 and 9?

d Divide 2610 by 45.

e Now check your answers with a calculator by using the **inverse** operation. Write the calculation first.

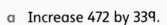

Remember!
+ is the inverse of −, and × is the inverse of ÷.

I can check an answer by working it backwards.

5.2 Number laws

1 Sanjay is checking the total number of pieces of fruit being laid out for a school lunch, to check that there is at least one serving of fruit per person.

Fill in the gaps and then find the total number of items on each table.

A 17 + _____ + 39 = ☐   _____ + 25 + 17 = ☐   25 + 39 + _____ = ☐

B 36 + 24 + 15 + _____ = ☐   12 + 15 + _____ + 36 = ☐

_____ + 24 + 15 + 12 = ☐   36 + _____ + 12 + 24 = ☐

What do you notice? Write a sentence about your findings. Make sure you mention **order**.

2 Write these numbers in four different orders:  Then multiply them together to find the answers. What do you notice?

☐ × ☐ × ☐ × ☐ = ☐   ☐ × ☐ × ☐ × ☐ = ☐

☐ × ☐ × ☐ × ☐ = ☐   ☐ × ☐ × ☐ × ☐ = ☐

3 Write the missing numbers and work out the answers.

a 4 × 16 = 4 × (10 + 6) = _4 × 10 + 4 × 6 = 40 + 24 = 64_

b 5 × 19 = 5 × (10 + 9) = 5 × _____ + 5 × _____ = 50 + _____ = ☐

c 9 × 35 = 9 × (_____ + _____) = _____ = ☐

4 Rearrange these numbers to make them easier to add.

a 14 + 29 + 16 = _(14 + 16) + 29 = 30 + 29 = 59_

b 24 + 15 + 25 = _____

c 9 + 36 + 41 = _____

d 38 + 27 + 42 = _____

Hint!
Look for pairs of numbers that add to multiples of ten.

I can change the order of numbers to make adding easier.

7.3 Outputs of functions in symbols

Cath's cafe

Coffee _____ 80p

Juice _____ 60p

Water _____ 50p

Muffin _____ 80p

Fruit _____ 40p

Sandwich 90p

1 Cath wants to find a quick way of recording the orders from her customers. She thinks **c** for coffee and **m** for muffins would be suitable. She writes two coffees and a muffin as **2c + m**.

Decide the best letters for the other items on the menu.

a juice _____

b water _____

c fruit _____

d sandwich _____

2 coffees   £1.60
sandwich   90p
muffin   80p
            _____
            £3.30

2 Write these orders using Cath's quick way.

a

b

c

d

a	b	c	d
	+		

3 Use the prices on the menu to work out the cost of each order in question 2. Record your answer as a number calculation. The first one has been done for you.

a   [3 × 60p]   =   [60p + 60p + 60p]   =   [£1.80]

b   [+   ]   =   [   ]

c   [2 ×   +   ]   =   [+   ]   =   [   ]

d   [3 ×   + 2 ×   ]   =   [+   ]   =   [   ]

4 Describe this picture using **s** for squares and **t** for triangles.

[+   ]

Hint!
c + c + c is the same as **3c**.

I can use symbols to express words.

7.4 Tables and coordinates

1 This graph shows the **4 times** and **6 times** multiplication tables.

The *x*-axis (along the bottom) shows what to multiply by and the *y*-axis (up the side) shows the answer.

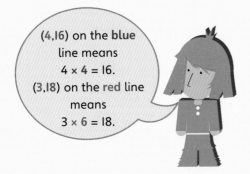

(4,16) on the **blue** line means 4 × 4 = 16.
(3,18) on the **red line** means 3 × 6 = 18.

Use the graph to find the answers to these multiplications.

a   5 × 4 = ☐

b   7 × 4 = ☐

c   9 × 4 = ☐

d $2\frac{1}{2}$ × 4 = ☐

e   4 × 6 = ☐

f   6 × 6 = ☐

g   8 × 6 = ☐

h $5\frac{1}{2}$ × 6 = ☐

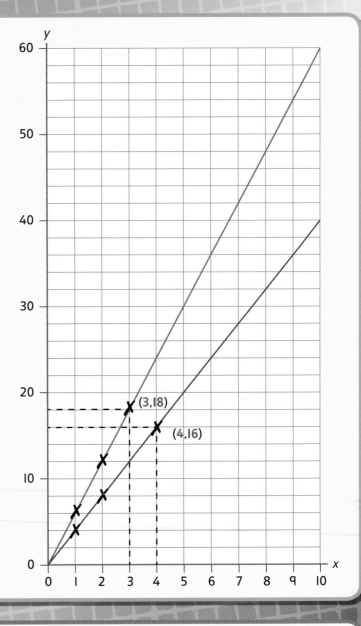

2 a Write the 9 times table in this table.

	1	2	3	4	5	6	7	8	9	10
× 9	9									

b To draw the 9 times table on a graph as in question 1, you need to make the numbers into coordinate pairs, for example, (1,9) and (2,18).

Complete these coordinates: (1 , ___)   (4 , ___)   (7 , ___)   (9 , ___)

3 Write the coordinates for the first four multiples of 5.

	1	2	3	4
× 5	5	10	15	20

(1 , ___)   (___ , ___)   (___ , ___)   (___ , ___)

I can make coordinate pairs from a table of data.

7.5 Straight line graphs

1 a Write the missing **output** numbers for this function machine. Then complete the table.

input numbers (*x*)

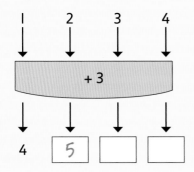

output numbers (*y*)

x + 3	x	1	2	3	4
	y	4			

b Now write the input (*x*) and output (*y*) numbers as (*x,y*) coordinate pairs.

(1, 4)   (2, ___)

(___ , ___)   (___ , ___)

c Plot the coordinates you have made on the grid. Then join up the points into a straight line. Continue the line upwards and then downwards until it meets the *y*-axis. Label the line *y = x + 3*.

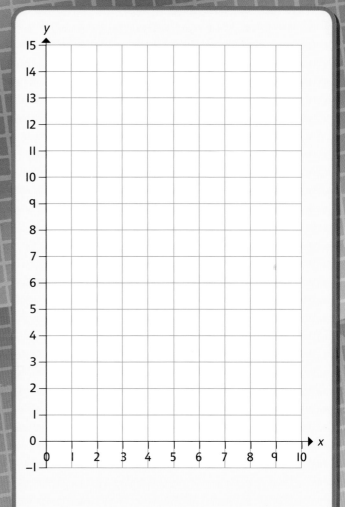

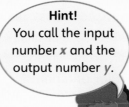
Hint!
You call the input number **x** and the output number **y**.

2 Complete the table for *y = x + 5* and plot the points on the grid. Join the points and label the line *y = x + 5*.

x + 5	x	0	1	2	3	4	5
	y						

3 Complete the table for *y = x − 1* and plot the points on the grid. Join the points and label the line *y = x − 1*.

x − 1	x	1	2	3	4	5
	y	0	1			

I can plot points from a table of values.

7.6 Interpreting real-life graphs

1 This real-life graph shows how many calories you burn when swimming.

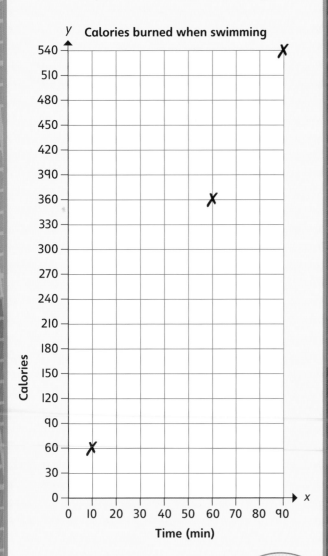

Calories burned when swimming

a Use a ruler and pencil to join the coordinates into a straight line.

b Continue the line downwards to the point (0,0).

The longer you swim, the more calories you burn.

2 Use the graph to find how many calories you can burn by swimming for:

a 20 min _____ calories

b 70 min _____ calories

c 45 min _____ calories

d 65 min _____ calories

3 Use the graph to find how many minutes you need to swim to burn:

a 240 calories _____ minutes

b 450 calories _____ minutes

4 a Mark the point (30,180) with a cross.

Is it on the line? Yes / No

Explain what this point means.

_____

_____

b Mark the point (80,380).

Is it on the line? Yes / No

Explain your answer.

_____

_____

5 Mark the points (20,150) and (60,450) with crosses on the graph. Join the points and continue the line to (0,0). This new line shows the calories burned in dancing.

a How many calories would you burn dancing for 40 minutes? _____

b What does the new line tell you?

_____

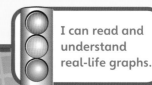

I can read and understand real-life graphs.

8.1 Rounding

1 a Estimate the numbers shown by the letters. Then round them to the nearest ten.

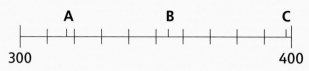

A |—|—|—|—|—|—|—|—|—|—|—| C
300   B   400

A | 317 | rounds to | 320 |
B | ☐ | rounds to | ☐ |
C | ☐ | rounds to | ☐ |

b Estimate the numbers shown by the letters. Then round them to the nearest hundred.

D   E   F
5000   6000

D | ☐ | rounds to | ☐ |
E | ☐ | rounds to | ☐ |
F | ☐ | rounds to | ☐ |

2 Round these numbers to the nearest thousand.
Colour the numbers that round to 3000.

What number have you made? _____

2871	3004	3499
2399	3567	2560
3723	2905	2504
2487	3602	3123
2602	3333	3450

3 Round each price to the nearest whole pound. Use the code to find a popular shopping place.

£4.80	£7.29	95p	35p	£3.99	£2.38	£5.55	£4.30	£2.61	49p	£7.56
£5										
S										

£0	£1	£2	£3	£4	£5	£6	£7	£8
E	P	M	K	R	S	A	U	T

4 Round each price to the nearest 10p.

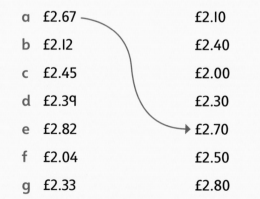

a   £2.67   £2.10

b   £2.12   £2.40

c   £2.45   £2.00

d   £2.39   £2.30

e   £2.82   £2.70

f   £2.04   £2.50

g   £2.33   £2.80

5 Round these amounts to the nearest whole pound.

a   £1.40 _____   b   £3.80 _____

c   £5.17 _____   d   £4.64 _____

I can round £.p amounts of money to the nearest whole pound.

8.2 Addition and subtraction

1 Complete the spider diagram so that opposite numbers add to 100.

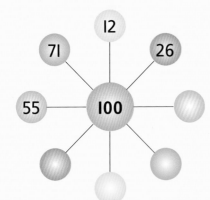

12

71   26

55   100

2 Write the answers. Make jottings on paper if you wish.

a   78 + 56 = ☐

b   78 − 49 = ☐

c   123 + 342 = ☐

d   546 − 208 = ☐

e   329 + 211 = ☐

f   301 − 199 = ☐

3 First, make an estimate. Then use column addition and subtraction to work out the answer.

a | 350 + 500 = 850 |

```
  3 4 5
  4 7 8 +
  8 2 3
  ₁ ₁
```

b | 550 − 300 = 250 |

```
  ⁴5 ¹³4̷ ⁶3̷
  2 7 6 −
  2 6 7
```

c | _____ |

```
  6 5 7
  2 7 4 +
```

d | _____ |

```
  3 9 6
  2 8 3 +
```

e | _____ |

```
  1 4 4 7
  2 7 2 5 +
```

f | _____ |

```
  8 2 4
  2 5 1 −
```

g | _____ |

```
  6 3 5
  3 7 8 −
```

h | _____ |

```
  3 7 1 4
  1 5 3 7 −
```

i   Write a subtraction you could use to check **c**.

j   Write an addition you could use to check **f**.

4 Work out the answers.

a
```
5 8 4
3 9 5 +
```

b
```
7 3 5
3 5 7 −
```

I can add and subtract 3-digit numbers.

8.3 Working with decimals 1

1 Quick practice! Work out the answers.

4.5 + 5.6 = [ ]　　　7.8 + 2.1 = [ ]　　　6.6 + 4.4 = [ ]　　　8.2 + 2.7 = [ ]

　　M　　　　　　　　　E　　　　　　　　　E　　　　　　　　　L

5.4 + 4.4 = [ ]　　　2.9 + 7.2 = [ ]　　　3.9 + 5.9 = [ ]　　　5.4 + 4.7 = [ ]

　　A　　　　　　　　　N　　　　　　　　　P　　　　　　　　　O

Collect the letters: answers < 10 _____　answers > 10 _____

Rearrange the letters to make the names of:

a fruit _____　　a vegetable _____

2 Dave can choose two piles of items to put in his holiday suitcase. The maximum weight allowed is 20 kg. Which combinations could he choose? Put a ring around **yes** or **no** for each combination.

A
11.45 kg

B
9.76 kg

C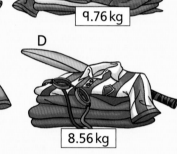
10.24 kg

D
8.56 kg

a　A + B
```
  1 1 . 4 5
    9 . 7 6 +
  _____
```
yes / no

b　B + C
```
    9 . 7 6
  1 0 . 2 4 +
  _____
```
yes / no

c　C + D
```
  1 0 . 2 4
    8 . 5 6 +
  _____
```
yes / no

d　A + C
```
  1 1 . 4 5
  1 0 . 2 4 +
  _____
```
yes / no

e　A + D
```
  1 1 . 4 5
    8 . 5 6 +
  _____
```
yes / no

f　B + D
```
    9 . 7 6
    8 . 5 6 +
  _____
```
yes / no

Remember!
Line up the decimal places carefully.

3 Multiply each number by 10 and 100.

	× 10	× 100		× 10	× 100
a　7			b　60		
c　480			d　3.7	37	
e　2.34	23.4		f　4.56		

4 What is the total? £4.79 + £5.36

I can add decimal numbers with 2 decimal places by putting them in columns.

8.4 Working with decimals 2

1 Quick practice! Find the answers in the grid and
cross them off. Which number is not crossed off? _____

5	6.7	2.2
1.9	5.3	5.7
8	2.7	7.2

   a   9.4 – 4.1   **b**   8.1 – 5.9   **c**   7.6 – 5.7   **d**   15.3 – 10.3

   e   10.2 – 7.5   **f**   15   – 7.8   **g**   17.6 – 9.6   **h**   21.6 – 15.9

2 Find out how much you save if you buy these items in the sale.
Work out an approximate answer using rounding first.

  a   **b**   **c**    **d**

£24.60   £50.50   £45.50   £75.75
£12.80   £24.99   £23.70   £32.80

a £25 – £13 = £12   **b**

     £ 2 4 . 6 0
     £ 1 2 . 8 0 –
     £ 1 1 . 8 0

c   **d**

e   Check your answers.

> **Hint!**
> Add the amount saved to the
> sale price: the total should be
> the original price.

3 Divide each number by 10 and 100.

	÷ 10	÷ 100		÷ 10	÷ 100
a 3000			**b** 74	7.4	
c 600			**d** 856		
e 30			**f** 360		

4 Ruth's packed suitcase weighs 19.6 kg.
The items inside weigh 16.8 kg.
What does the empty suitcase weigh?
Use column subtraction to find out.

I can subtract
with decimal
numbers.

8.5 Multiplication

1 a Work out the value of each letter and complete the table.

$4 \times a = 12$ $6 \times b = 36$ $c \times 4 = 28$ $d \times 9 = 36$

$3 \times e = 27$ $f \times 7 = 35$ $5 \times g = 40$ $8 \times h = 80$

a	b	c	d	e	f	g	h
3							

Now use the letter values and work out the mystery calculations.

b $g \times a =$ [8 × 3] = [24]   **c** $a \times c =$ [×] = [ ]

d $d \times f =$ [×] = [ ]   **e** $h \times b =$ [×] = [ ]

f $e \times h =$ [×] = [ ]   **g** $c \times f =$ [×] = [ ]

---

2 **Partition** these numbers to multiply.

a $24 \times 6 = (\underline{20} \times \underline{6}) + (\underline{4} \times \underline{6}) = \boxed{120} + \boxed{24} = \boxed{144}$

b $32 \times 4 = (\underline{} \times \underline{}) + (\underline{} \times \underline{}) = \boxed{} + \boxed{} = \boxed{}$

c $45 \times 9 = (\underline{} \times \underline{}) + (\underline{} \times \underline{}) = \boxed{} + \boxed{} = \boxed{}$

d $28 \times 5 = (\underline{} \times \underline{}) + (\underline{} \times \underline{}) = \boxed{} + \boxed{} = \boxed{}$

---

3 Work out these multiplications using the grid method.

a 235×4

×	200	30	5	
4	800			=

b 172×5

×	100	70	2	
5				=

c 463×3

×				

---

4 Use the grid method to work out 295×6.

I can multiply HTU by U using a grid.

8.6 Factors and multiples

1 a Which number does each symbol represent? Fill in the table.

$21 \div \bigstar = 7$ $15 \div \heartsuit = 3$ $28 \div \maltese = 4$ $42 \div \smiley = 7$

$21 \div 3 = 7$

$24 \div \clubsuit = 3$ $42 \div \bullet = 21$ $40 \div \blacksquare = 10$ $45 \div \blacktriangle = 5$

$\bigstar$	$\heartsuit$	$\maltese$	$\smiley$	$\clubsuit$	$\bullet$	$\blacksquare$	$\blacktriangle$
3							

Use the same values to work out these calculations

b $\bigstar \times \clubsuit = \bigcirc$ **c** $\blacksquare \times \blacktriangle = \bigcirc$ **d** $\blacktriangle \div \bigstar = \bigcirc$ **e** $\clubsuit \div \bullet = \bigcirc$

2 Write on each keypad the digits 1–9 that are **factors** of the number in the display screen.

a 400   b 420   c 360   d 280   e 250

3 Complete these sentences.

a 236 is a multiple of 2 because _____

b 236 is **not** a multiple of 5 because _____

c 236 is **not** a multiple of 9 because _____

d 312 is a multiple of _____, _____, _____, _____, _____ and _____

> **Tip!**
> If a number is a factor of 18, then it is also a factor of 180, 1800 and other multiples of 18.

I can use tests of divisibility.

8.7 Division

1 a Write the first ten multiples of 25. The first two have been done for you.

<u>25</u>, <u>50</u>, ____, ____, ____, ____, ____, ____, ____, ____

b What do you notice about the multiples of 25?

_____

c Complete the multiplication facts. Join each multiplication to its related division fact. Then complete the division facts.

4 × 25 = ☐   250 ÷ 25 = ☐

7 × 25 = ☐   125 ÷ 25 = ☐

10 × 25 = ☐   100 ÷ 25 = ☐

3 × 25 = ☐   175 ÷ 25 = ☐

8 × 25 = ☐   75 ÷ 25 = ☐

5 × 25 = ☐   200 ÷ 25 = ☐

Hint!
24 ÷ 6 = 4
because
4 × 6 = 24.

---

2 Use division facts to find the answers.

a
$$\begin{array}{r} 3 \\ 2\overline{)\ 6\ 8\ 4} \end{array}$$

b
$$3\overline{)\ 6\ 9\ 3}$$

c
$$5\overline{)\ 5\ 1\ 5}$$

d
$$4\overline{)\ 2\ 4\ 8}$$

e
$$3\overline{)\ 2\ 5\ 2}$$

f
$$6\overline{)\ 2\ 8\ 8}$$

---

3 Shade the divisions that have a remainder in the answer.

What letter have you made? _____

24 ÷ 5	30 ÷ 7	32 ÷ 3
28 ÷ 9	25 ÷ 5	28 ÷ 4
36 ÷ 8	40 ÷ 3	24 ÷ 7
40 ÷ 6	40 ÷ 8	36 ÷ 9
29 ÷ 9	51 ÷ 5	72 ÷ 10

4 Find the answer using division.

$$4\overline{)\ 3\ 6\ 8}$$

I can divide 3-digit
numbers by a
single-digit number.

8.8 Using a calculator 1

1 What answer is on the display at the end?

a [45] [+] [78] [CE] [+] [87] [=] ▢

b [3] [×] [5] [+] [17] [CE] [=] ▢

c [20] [÷] [4] [+] [7] [CE] [−] [7] [+] [2] [=] ▢

d What does the CE key do? _____

2 Write brackets to make these calculations correct.

a 24.5 + 17.9 × 4.5 = 105.05

b 83.6 ÷ 12.3 − 6.8 = 15.2

c 15.6 × 12.4 − 9.8 = 183.64

d 57.9 − 23.5 × 10.4 = 357.76

> **Remember!**
> Clear the memory before you start a new calculation.

3 Find the answers to these calculations. Then join pairs with the same answer.

(15.7 − 7.6) × 10

7 [x^2]

5 × 5

64 ÷ 8

7.6 + (3.2 × 5.4)

7 × 7

5 [x^2]

64 [√]

3.2 × 5.4 + 7.6

9 [x^2]

4 Find the answers using a calculator.

> **Tip!**
> Practise using the keys on your calculator so you know how to use them in calculations.

a 187.24 ÷ (6.3 + 12.4 − 3.6) = ▢

b (27.34 − 17.89) × (12.6 ÷ 3) = ▢

> I can use the brackets keys on the calculator.

8.9 Using a calculator 2

1 Use your calculator to work these out. Draw lines to the correct answer.

a [12.8] [–] [2.9] [M+] [4.2] [×] [MRC] [=]

b [12.8] [–] [( ] [2.9] [×] [4.2] [ )] [=]

c [( ] [12.8] [–] [2.9] [ )] [×] [4.2] [=]

41.58

0.62

2 Use a calculator to check if 11, 13 or 17 are factors of these numbers.

Draw a tick (✓) for factors and a cross (✗) for non-factors.

		11	13	17
a	312			
b	306			
c	495			
d	221			
e	748			
f	2431		✓	

2431 ÷ 13 = 187

Tip!
Dividing a number by a **factor** gives a whole number answer.

3 Answer these problems using a calculator. Write the calculation.

a What is the total cost of eight CDs at £12.99 each?

b What is the sum of the first seven odd numbers?

3, 9, 5, 13, 1, 11, 7

c T-shirts cost £15. How many can I buy with £100?

d How much less is the special offer price?

£169.99 special offer price £124.49

e 645 pupils and teachers go to a theme park. Coaches carry 53 passengers. How many coaches will be needed?

4 Tom buys items for £2.56, £3.04 and £12. How much change will he get from £20?

I can use a calculator and interpret the display.

9.1 Symmetry

1 a  b c d e f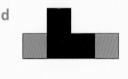

Draw the lines of symmetry on each road sign. Complete the table.

	a	b	c	d	e	f
Number of lines of symmetry						

2 Draw one more black square on each shape to make a new shape with symmetry.

Use a dotted line to show the line of symmetry.

a   b 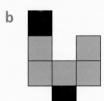   c   d

_____   _____   _____   _____

Say whether the line of symmetry in each shape is horizontal, vertical or diagonal.

3 Draw lines of symmetry on these triangles.

a   b    c

Complete the table.

	Type of triangle	Number of lines of symmetry
a		
b		
c		

4 Draw the lines of symmetry on these shapes.

a   b   c   d

What do you notice about these regular polygons?

I can recognise and draw lines of symmetry in shapes.

9.2 Reflection

1 Which drawings show reflections? _____

A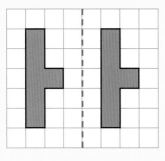

B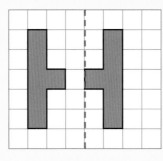

C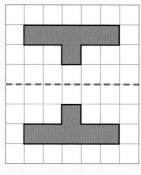

D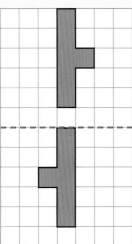

E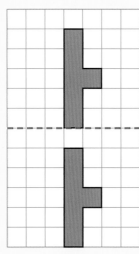

F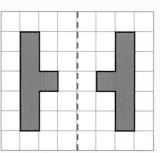

2 Draw yellow squares so that each diagram shows a reflection in the red mirror line.

a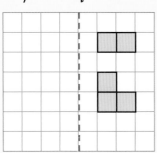

b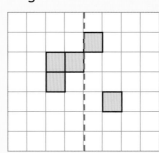

c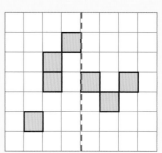

3 Reflect each shape on to the other side of the mirror line.

a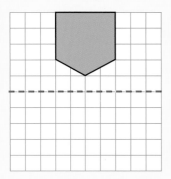

b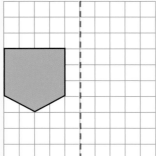

c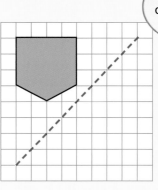

You may use a mirror to help you.

I can reflect a shape in a mirror line.

9.3 Translation

1 Which statement correctly describes the translation from the red shape to the blue shape? _____

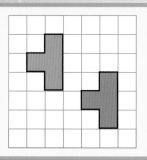

   a Slide the red shape 2 squares right, 1 down

   b Slide the red shape 3 squares right, 2 down

   c Slide the red shape 3 squares right, 1 down

2 Describe these translations. Draw your translations on the grid and write the instructions below.

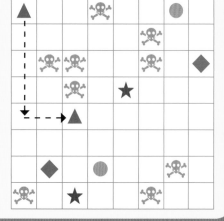

The ☠ squares are NO-GO areas!

My translations:

▲   4 down, 2 right _____

★ _____

◆ _____

● _____

3 Move each shape using the given translations.

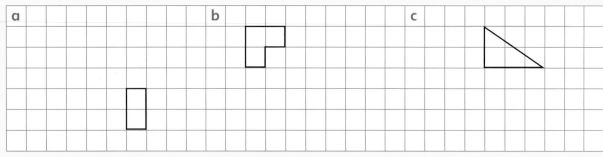

   3 squares left   3 squares right   2 squares left
   2 squares up   2 squares down   3 squares down

4 a Describe the translation from rectangle A to rectangle B.

    _____

  b Draw the image of rectangle B after a translation 3 squares right and 4 up.

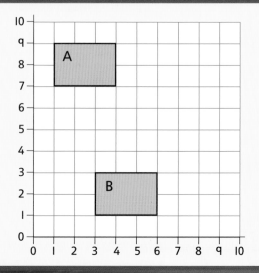

I understand and can describe translations.

9.4 Rotation

1 Describe the rotation of each blue shape to the green shape.

Use some of these words:

clockwise   anti-clockwise   quarter turn   half turn   three-quarter turn

a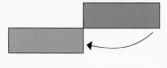

_____

b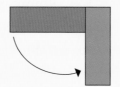

_____

c

_____

2 Rotate each shape on the grid and then complete the table to show the new coordinates.

A half clockwise turn around (2,4)

B quarter anti-clockwise turn around (9,9)

C three-quarter clockwise turn around (7,2)

Shape	New coordinates
A	
B	
C	

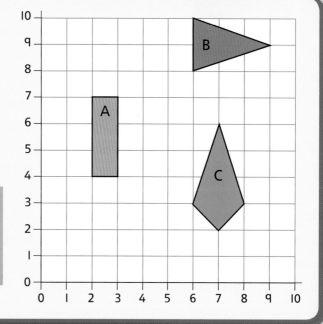

3 Draw where each shape will be after the size of turn given.

a clockwise half turn

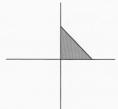

b clockwise quarter turn

c anti-clockwise quarter turn

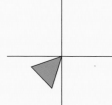

d anti-clockwise three-quarter turn

I can recognise where a shape will be after a rotation.

9.5 Combining transformations

1 Follow the instructions and see what happens!

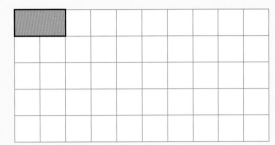

a Translate the rectangle 2 squares to the right and I down. Colour it red.

b Rotate it clockwise a quarter of a turn around its bottom right-hand corner. Colour it blue.

c Reflect the blue shape in a mirror line at its base. Colour it green.

d Reflect the whole pattern in a mirror line on the right of the blue and green rectangles. Colour the shape to make it symmetrical.

2 Look at the shapes in this grid. How have the separate triangle, square and pentagon moved to make the new combined shape?

Use the words **reflect**, **translate** or **rotate** to describe the movement of each shape.

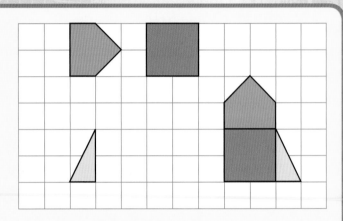

a Triangle _____

b Square _____

c Pentagon _____

3 a Which squares are a rotation of D? _____

b Which squares are a rotation of A? _____

c Draw a line of symmetry on the grid.

d Describe how you could translate A to E. _____

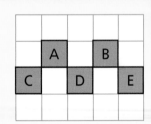

4 Describe each transformation.

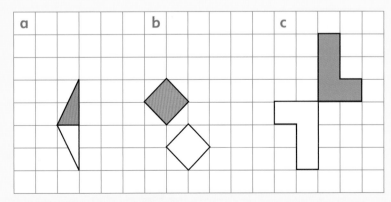

a _____

b _____

c _____

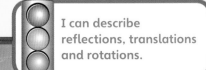

I can describe reflections, translations and rotations.

9.6 Solving problems

1 Here are two right-angled isosceles triangles.

Hint!
You can make three shapes.

   a Visualise the shapes that you can make if the triangles touch along a side.

   Draw and name the shapes.

   b Describe the transformations of the triangles that make your new shapes.

2 Use these instructions to design a new wallpaper pattern.

- The wallpaper should be made of **congruent** right-angled isosceles triangles.

- The pattern must reflect in either a vertical or a horizontal mirror line.

- All the triangles must be transformations of the first one that you draw.

Draw your design on the grid.

Describe your first transformation.

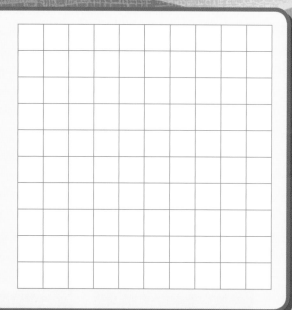

3 The dance troupe Fancy Feet have made themselves into a star shape.

Using only **clockwise rotations**, describe how to get from one position to another:

   a from A to C   _____

   b from B to A   _____

   c from C to D   _____

   d Draw lines of symmetry on the shape they have made. How many are there?

   _____

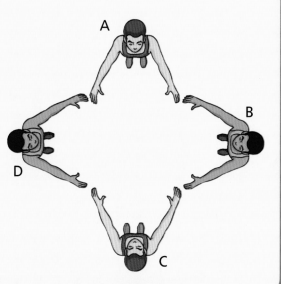

I can solve problems using reflections, rotations and translations.

10.1 Rules of operations

1 Complete these families of four facts.

   a $23 + 45 = 68$ $45 + \boxed{} = 68$ **b** $35 \times 22 = 770$ $22 \times \boxed{} = 770$

        $68 - 23 = \boxed{}$ $68 - \boxed{} = 23$ $770 \div 35 = \boxed{}$ $\boxed{} \div 22 = \boxed{}$

2 Use a calculator to find the missing numbers.

X	
Y	
Z	
H	
J	
K	

   $24.5 + X = 58.3$ $75.2 - Y = 26.3$ $Z - 14.7 = 29.6$

   $15 \times H = 375$ $J \times 24 = 384$ $300 \div K = 25$

Use the values to work out and write the codes on the safes.

   a $X + (Y + Z)$ **b** $(H \times J) \times K$ **c** $H \times (Y - Z + K)$

  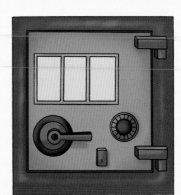

3 Spot which calculations have the same answers. Draw lines to join them.
Check with a calculator.

   24×12 $26 + 80 + 15$ $(27 - 14) \times 6$

   $15 + (26 + 80)$ $6 \times (27 - 14)$ $(12 \times 20) + (12 \times 4)$

   $(27 \times 6) - (14 \times 6)$ 12×24 $(15 + 26) + 80$

4 Work out the missing numbers.

   a $2 \times M = 30$ **b** $270 \div N = 30$

      $M = \boxed{}$ $N = \boxed{}$

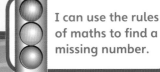

I can use the rules
of maths to find a
missing number.

10.2 Order of operations

1 Write the answers to these calculations.

a 7 + 3 × 4 = ☐

b 20 − 6 × 2 = ☐

c 24 − 16 ÷ 4 = ☐

d 5 × 8 ÷ 4 = ☐

e 20 ÷ 5 + 15 = ☐

f 3 × 4 + 5 × 6 = ☐

g 20 ÷ 5 + 2 × 6 = ☐

h 2 × 8 − 3 × 5 = ☐

> **Remember!**
> Do multiplication and division before addition and subtraction.

2 Work out the answers to these calculations. Use the brackets or memory keys on a calculator.

Example: You can do 12 × (3.5 + 6.2) as:

a 16 × (4.8 − 2.3) = ☐

b 250 ÷ (23.2 + 26.8) = ☐

c 50 × (29.5 − 16.7) ÷ 40 = ☐

d 180 ÷ (14.3 + 15.7) × 10 = ☐

3 a Farmer Holland's 24 chickens each lay an average of 8 eggs every week.

How many 12-egg trays does he need each week to pack them?

Ring the calculation needed to solve this word problem.

24 × 8 × 12   24 × 12 ÷ 8   24 ÷ 12 ÷ 8   24 × 8 ÷ 12

Now use your calculator to work out the answer.

_____

b Three brothers have been saving their pocket money. Dad says that he will double what they save and then add £10 to the total. Ben has saved £6.50, Dan £6.25 and Chris £6.40.

Ring the calculation that shows how much they will have altogether.

(6.50 + 6.25 + 6.40 + 10) × 2   2 × (6.50 + 6.25 + 6.40 + 10)

(6.50 + 6.25 + 6.40) × 2 + 10   2 × 10 + (6.50 + 6.25 + 6.40)

Now use your calculator to work out the answer.

_____

4 Write the answers.

a 12 − 2 × 5 = ☐

b 6 + 4 ÷ 2 = ☐

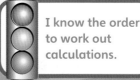

> I know the order to work out calculations.

10.3 Square and triangle numbers

1 a Continue the pattern. Then write the sequence of **square numbers**.

1×1	2×2	3×3	4×4	$5 \times \underline{}$	$6 \times \underline{}$
1^2	2^2	3^2	___	___	___
1	4	9	☐	☐	☐

b Use the key on your calculator to work out the next square numbers.

$7 \times 7 = \quad 7^2 = $ ☐ $\qquad 8 \times 8 = $ ____ $ = $ ☐

$9 \times 9 = $ ____ $ = $ ☐ $\qquad 10 \times 10 = $ ____ $ = $ ☐

c Write the missing square numbers.

81 ☐ 49 36 ☐ ☐ 9 4 ☐

---

2 a Continue the pattern of triangles. Complete the number sentences.

 1
   1

 $1 + 2$
 3

 $1 + 2 + 3$
 ___

$1 + 2 + $ ____ $ + $ ____

____

$1 + 2 + $ _____

____

$1 + 2 + $ _____

____

b Write the first 10 **triangle numbers**. Use a calculator to find the last four.

1   3

---

3 Explain how to work out square numbers.

 I can explain how to work out square numbers.

10.4 More sequences

1 Which is which? Match the sequence to the rule.

a   1, 4, 9, 16, 25, ...   triangle numbers

b   1, 5, 9, 13, 17, ...   double, add 1

c   1, 3, 7, 15, 31, ...   square numbers

d   1, 3, 6, 10, 15, ...   add 4

e   4, 8, 12, 16, 20, ...   multiples of 4

2 Work out the rule for each sequence. Then write in the missing numbers.

a   7,   8.5,   10,   11.5,   _____, _____, _____   Rule: _____

b   _____, _____, 24,   21,   18,   _____, _____   Rule: _____

c   27,   39,   _____, 63,   _____, _____, _____   Rule: _____

d   1.2,   _____, 1.6,   1.8,   _____, _____, _____   Rule: _____

e   5.3,   4.8,   _____, 3.8,   3.3,   _____, _____   Rule: _____

3 Write the first five terms of the following sequences.

a   Start at 5. Rule: add 11.   _____

b   Start at 99. Rule: subtract 9.   _____

c   Start at 40. Rule: halve.   _____

d   Start at 1.5 Rule: add 0.2   _____

e   Start at 5. Rule: double.   _____

4 Work out the rule and write in the missing numbers.

480, 240, 120, _____, _____, _____   Rule: _____

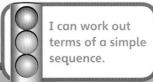

I can work out terms of a simple sequence.

10.5 Complex sequences

1 Write the missing numbers on these scales – the numbers follow a sequence.
Work out what each interval (gap between numbers) is worth.

a

Interval: _____

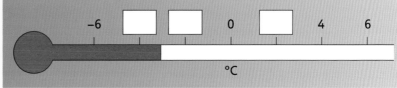

−6 [ ] [ ] 0 [ ] 4 6

°C

b

Interval: _____

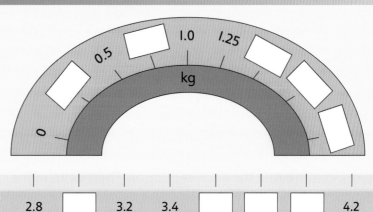

0.5 1.0 1.25
kg
0

c

Interval: _____

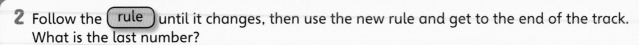

2.8 [ ] 3.2 3.4 [ ] [ ] [ ] 4.2

cm

2 Follow the (rule) until it changes, then use the new rule and get to the end of the track.
What is the last number?

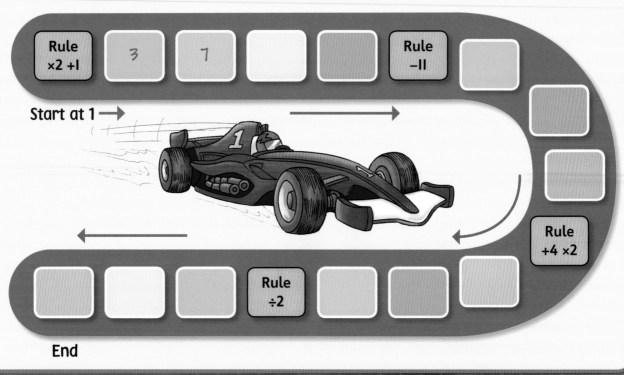

Rule
×2 +1

3   7

Rule
−11

Start at 1 →

Rule
+4 ×2

Rule
÷2

End

3 Write the first four terms of this sequence.

Start at 0. Rule: +3 ×2.   _____, _____, _____, _____

I can follow a
rule to continue
a sequence.

10.6 Number puzzles

1 Use the x^2 key on a calculator to find the numbers.

Fill in the table to find the secret PIN number.

$P^2 = 225$ $I^2 = 529$ $N^2 = 961$

P	I	N

2 Find the missing numbers.

Hint!
1, 2, 3 and
6, 7, 8 are sets
of **consecutive**
numbers.

a   The **same** number is missing.
☐ × ☐ × ☐ = 729

b   **Consecutive** numbers are missing.
☐ × ☐ × ☐ = 210

c   Use multiples of 10 only.
☐ + ☐ + ☐ = 350

3 Use column addition or subtraction to solve these word problems.

a   There are 375 girls and 516 boys.
How many more boys are there?

b   What is the distance from Miami to Atlanta?

229miles   428 miles

Miami   Orlando   Atlanta

c   What is the total length of the rope?

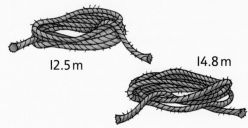

12.5 m   14.8 m

d   What is the difference in price?

£41.50

£24.89

4 Use a calculator to work out the missing number.

The **same** number is missing.   ☐ × ☐ = 289

I can use a
calculator to solve
number puzzles.

11.1 Collecting data

1 Fill the gaps in this tally chart.

Favourite fruit	Tally	Frequency
Apple	卌 ‖	
Pear	‖	
Orange		3
Grapes	卌 卌 卌		
Melon		12
Strawberry		9

2 This list shows 30 pupils' favourite football teams.

City	City	United	United	Athletic	Rovers
United	Town	Albion	Albion	City	United
Town	Athletic	City	United	Albion	Rovers
City	United	Athletic	United	Town	United
United	Rovers	City	Rovers	City	Albion

Record the data in a frequency table.

Favourite team	Tally	Frequency

3 You want to find out which video games are most popular with ten of your friends.

Design a data collection sheet to help you find out, and then collect the information that will help you answer the question.

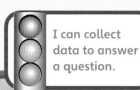

I can collect data to answer a question.

11.2 Range and mode

1   At the Woodside Darts Championships, Catherine and two friends get the following scores with their first three darts:

Catherine: 38   15   20

Brian: 7   18   12

Mary: 27   34   50

What is the range of all their scores? _____

2   In a Twenty-20 cricket match, the players in Jo's team scored the following runs:

10   5   19   12   20   2   9   36   14   3   17

What is the range of the scores? _____

3   a   The last 12 customers in a shoe shop bought shoes in these sizes:

$4\frac{1}{2}$ 8 $5\frac{1}{2}$ 5   7   7 $5\frac{1}{2}$ $6\frac{1}{2}$ 4   8 $5\frac{1}{2}$ 6

Which shoe size is the mode? _____

   b   The last 12 customers at a hardware shop bought these tins of paint:

white	blue	red	blue	green	brown
white	white	red	white	orange	white

Which colour paint is the mode? _____

4   Sophie's hockey team scored this number of goals in their first ten games:

3   2   0   2   4   1   5   2   0   6

   a   What is the range of the number of goals scored?

_____

   b   What is the mode of the number of goals scored?

_____

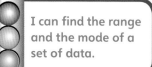
I can find the range and the mode of a set of data.

11.3 Median and mean

1 Aden, Ben and Rajeev sprint 80 metres five times each. Their times in seconds are:

Aden: 10   12   14   9   13

Ben: 8   12   14   15   11

Rajeev: 14   11   15   17   12

What is the median time of each runner?

Aden: _____

Ben: _____

Rajeev: _____

2 The table shows the rainfall collected in three towns during the first six months of the year.

Town	Jan	Feb	Mar	April	May	June
Templecombe	9 mm	12 mm	15 mm	4 mm	13 mm	7 mm
Longbarrow	13 mm	20 mm	8 mm	9 mm	17 mm	11 mm
Ravenscrag	5 mm	14 mm	9 mm	6 mm	16 mm	4 mm

> **Hint!**
> To find the mean, add the values and divide by the number of values.

a   What is the median rainfall in each town?

Templecombe _____

Longbarrow _____

Ravenscrag _____

b   Which town has the highest mean rainfall?

c   Which town has the lowest mean rainfall?

3 A van driver records the distances he travels for 3 weeks.
For each week write the distances in order. Then write in and circle the median.

	Monday	Tuesday	Wednesday	Thursday	Friday	Saturday
Week 1	30 km	24 km	15 km	27 km	19 km	24 km
Week 2	41 km	29 km	12 km	36 km	25 km	19 km
Week 3	53 km	24 km	38 km	46 km	20 km	37 km

Week 1 _____

Week 2 _____

Week 3 _____

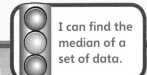

I can find the median of a set of data.

11.4 Pictograms and bar charts

1 A music store recorded the CD sales of five popular groups.

   a The Enemies sold 25 CDs. Draw this information on the pictogram.

   b Which group sold the most CDs?

       _____

   c How many more did the Kestrels sell than the Spuds? _____

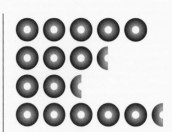

Group

Kestrels
Planets
Spuds
Tridents
Enemies

⬤ = 10 CDs

2 This dual bar chart shows the sales of coffee and tea at Susie's Snack Bar from Monday to Friday.

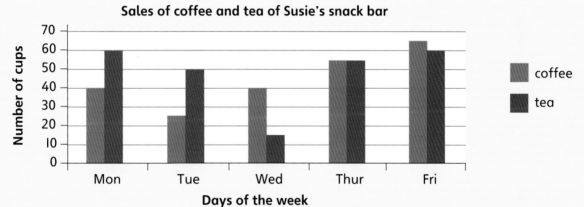

Sales of coffee and tea of Susie's snack bar

   a On which day were most coffees sold? _____ How many? _____

   b On which day were least teas sold? _____ How many? _____

   c How many drinks were sold on Friday? _____

   d On which day did the snack bar sell equal numbers of tea and coffee? _____

3 This table shows the shoe sizes of 20 pupils.

Shoe size	Frequency
1–2	2
3–4	6
5–6	8
7–8	4

Draw a bar chart to represent this data.

I can draw bar charts.

11.5 Line graphs

1 This line graph shows the annual average monthly temperatures in Edinburgh and Sydney.

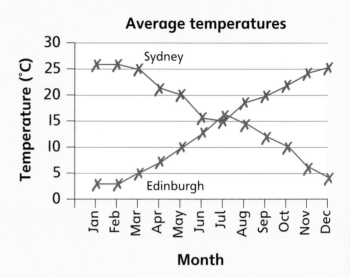

Average temperatures

a When are the warmest months in Sydney? _____

b When is the warmest month in Edinburgh? _____

c What is the average temperature in each city in March?

Sydney: _____

Edinburgh: _____

d When is the average temperature in Edinburgh higher than it is in Sydney?

_____

e Write a sentence describing the information in the graph.

_____

2 This line graph shows the votes cast for the Red Party in the last six elections.

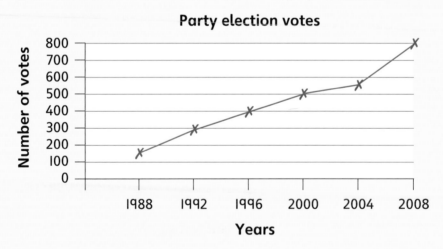

Party election votes

a Plot these results for the Blue Party on the same axes.

1988	1992	1996	2000	2004	2008
300	200	500	350	350	150

b Circle the point on the graph where the Blue Party got their lowest vote.

c How many votes in total did the Red Party get in 2000 and 2004? _____

d In which years did the Blue Party do better than the Red Party? _____

e Which party has grown steadily in popularity? _____

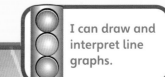

I can draw and interpret line graphs.

11.6 Pie charts

1 This pie chart shows the type of homes 24 people live in.

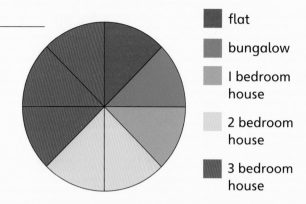

a How many people live in a flat? _____

b How many people live in a 2-bedroom house? _____

c How many people live in a 3-bedroom house? _____

d How many people do not live in a bungalow? _____

Key:
- flat
- bungalow
- 1 bedroom house
- 2 bedroom house
- 3 bedroom house

2 Draw a pie chart to show the favourite type of music chosen by some pupils. Write three sentences about the information shown.

Type of music	Frequency
Reggae	4
Garage	2
Hip hop	2
Rap	1
Heavy metal	7
Total	16

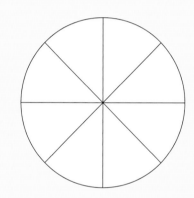

Remember!
Give the pie chart a title and a key.

3 These pie charts show the results of 24 hockey matches played by two local schools.

a Who won more matches?

_____

b Who drew more matches?

_____

c How many games did Southwick School win? _____

d Which team has the worse record?

_____

Southwick School

lost
won
drawn

Northport School

won
lost
drawn

I can interpret pie charts.

Revision

Quick quiz

1 a Use rounding to estimate the answer to 68 × 7.

_____

b Calculate 68 × 7.

→ *See 8.1, 8.5*

2 These coordinates are three corners of a rectangle: (1,2), (1,4), (4,2)

a Plot these points on the grid.

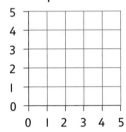

b What are the coordinates of the fourth corner of the rectangle?

_____

→ *See 7.1*

3 a What is the fourth square number? _____

b What is the fourth triangle number? _____

→ *See 10.3*

4 Reflect this triangle in the line of symmetry.

→ *See 9.2*

5 a Find the sum of 275 and 146.

b Find the difference between 275 and 146.

→ *See 8.2*

6 Use the graph to convert between miles and kilometres.

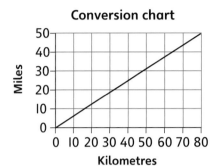

a 15 miles = _____ km

b 50 km = _____ miles

→ *See 7.6, 11.5*

7 a Draw all the lines of symmetry in these two triangles.

_____   _____

b Write the special names of these triangles.

→ *See 9.1*

8 Add the numbers that are below 8.

6.92   9.13   14.2   8.4   5.27

_____

→ *See 8.3*

9 Describe this transformation fully.

→ *See 9.4*

10 Here are the heights, in metres, of seven pupils in Jo's class. What is the median height?

1.62   1.45   1.56   1.47   1.62   1.55   1.59

_____

→ *See 11.3*

Revision

Check up questions

1 **a** Translate rectangle A 2 squares to the right and I square down.

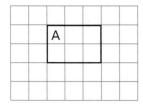

  b Draw the lines of symmetry in rectangle A.

→ *See 9.1, 9.3*

2 A shop decides to stock some new 'Healthy Start' breakfast cereals. The frequency table shows the number of packets sold during the first afternoon of sale.

  a Complete the table.

New cereals	Number of packets sold
Orangey Oats	12
Raisin Rye	8
Carrotty Corn	
TOTAL	31

  b Which cereal was the most popular that afternoon?

_____

→ *See 11.4*

3 Here are three numbers: 173 429 356

  a Choose the two numbers that will give the biggest total possible. Add them.

  b Choose the two numbers that have the biggest difference. Subtract the smaller one from the larger one.

→ *See 8.2*

4 Eight leaves have the following lengths (in cm):

9.24 7.1 5.12 9.24 3.67 5.62 6.66 6.62

  a What does the word **average** mean?

_____

  b What length is the **mode**?

_____

  c What length is the **median**?

_____

  d Which do you think is the better average to use in this case? Explain why.

→ *See 11.2, 11.3*

5 **a** Find a number which is both a square number and a triangle number.

_____

  b A sequence has this rule: Multiply the number before by 3 and subtract 10.

  Write the next two terms in the sequence.

17, 41, _____, _____

→ *See 10.3, 10.4*

6 **a** Round 87 to the nearest ten. _____

  Round 376 to the nearest hundred.

_____

  b By rounding these numbers to the nearest ten, estimate the answer to:

$(47 + 12) \times 8$

→ *See 8.1, 10.2*

Activity: At the Superstore

You will need: centimetre squared paper.

1 Darren is making tins of cat food into a display, but he is also thinking about the patterns he can make.

I tin   3 tins   _____ tins

a Write how many tins he used in the third pile.

b Draw the fourth pile. How many tins did he use in this pile?

_____

c Write out and continue the sequence for seven piles.

I, 3, 6, _____, _____, _____, _____,

d What is the name of this sequence?

_____

→ *See 10.3, 10.4*

2 a Darren's manager wants three of the 5-high piles along the front of the shop and four of the 8-high piles along the back wall of the store. How many tins will these displays use?

b The tins come in boxes of 24. How many boxes will Darren need for these displays?

→ *See 8.2, 8.5, 8.7, 8.8*

3 Rita has been asked to design a range of bed linen. She likes Darren's stacks of cans and decides to use the same idea in her designs. Her first three designs are:

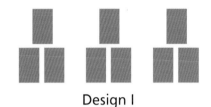

Design I

Design 2

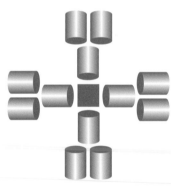

Design 3

a Describe, in as much detail as possible, each of Rita's designs. Use the words **reflection**, **rotation** and **translation** in your descriptions.

Design I: _____

_____

Design 2: _____

_____

Design 3: _____

_____

b Design a border, with a symbol or picture of your choice, using at least one type of transformation (reflection, rotation, translation). Draw it on centimetre squared paper.

→ *See 9.2–9.5*

12.1 Multiplication and division

1 Use the **grid method** to multiply these numbers.

   a 398 × 6

       approximate answer = _____

×	300	90	8	
6				

   b 407 × 8

       approximate answer = _____

Use the **column method** to work out these multiplications.

   c 3 9 8
        6 ×

   d 4 0 7
        8 ×

   e 7 9 6
        3 ×

   f 8 1 4
        4 ×

   g Compare the answers to **c** and **e**, and to **d** and **f**.

       Explain what has happened.

Hint!
What is double 398?

2 Work out the answers to these division calculations.

   a

      6) 3 4 2

   b

      7) 2 5 9

   c

      8) 4 9 6

   d

      9) 5 7 2 4

4 Choose a division from question 3 that does not have a remainder. Work out the answer.

)

I can do division.

3 Some of these divisions have a **remainder**. Use a calculator or tests of divisibility to find which have a remainder and which do not, and complete the table.

Division	Remainder	
	Yes	No
a 3756 ÷ 5		
b 4362 ÷ 3		
c 3857 ÷ 6		
d 4732 ÷ 4		
e 2376 ÷ 8		
f 2483 ÷ 9		

12.2 Fractions, decimals, percentages

1 Mark all these fractions, decimals and percentages on the correct number line.

$\frac{1}{10}$　30%　90%　$\frac{3}{10}$　$\frac{9}{10}$　25%　0.75　0.25

0.1　$\frac{3}{4}$　0.9　75%　$\frac{1}{4}$　10%　0.3

a

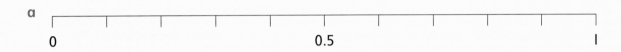

0 　　　　　　　0.5　　　　　　　1

b

0 　　　　　　　$\frac{1}{2}$　　　　　　　1

c

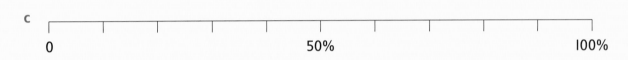

0 　　　　　　　50%　　　　　　100%

Complete the table.

d Write the equivalent trios.

e Tick whether each trio is less than, equal to or more than $\frac{1}{2}$.

A **trio** is a group of three.

Percentage	Fraction	Decimal	$< \frac{1}{2}$	$= \frac{1}{2}$	$> \frac{1}{2}$
50%	$\frac{1}{2}$	0.5		✓	
	$\frac{1}{10}$				
		0.75			
	$\frac{1}{4}$				
		0.3			
90%					

2 Use a calculator to change these fractions into decimals and percentages. Join up the equivalent values.

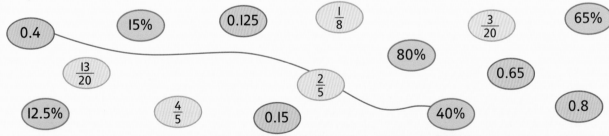

0.4　15%　0.125　$\frac{1}{8}$　$\frac{3}{20}$　65%
$\frac{13}{20}$　　　　　80%　　0.65
12.5%　$\frac{4}{5}$　0.15　$\frac{2}{5}$　40%　0.8

3 a 　$\frac{1}{4}$ = ⬭ % = ⬭

b ⬭ = 70% = ⬭

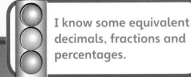

I know some equivalent decimals, fractions and percentages.

12.3 More about fractions

1 a Colour the pie chart to match the key. Identify the fraction of the yellow section.

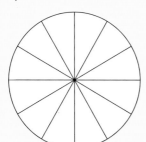

 $\frac{1}{3}$

□ $\frac{1}{4}$

□ $\frac{1}{6}$

□ $\boxed{\dfrac{}{}}$

b Complete the equivalent fractions.

$$\frac{1}{3} = \frac{\Box}{12}$$ $$\frac{1}{4} = \frac{\Box}{12}$$

$$\frac{1}{6} = \frac{\Box}{12}$$

---

2 Use the diagrams to add and subtract fractions.

a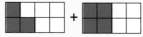

□ + □ = □

b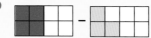

□ − □ = □

c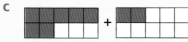

□ + □ = □

d

□ − □ = □

---

3 Find these fractions of amounts. Check your answers with a calculator.

Fraction	Amount		
	80	£20	400 ml
a $\frac{1}{2}$			
b $\frac{1}{10}$			
c $\frac{1}{5}$			
d $\frac{1}{4}$			
e $\frac{3}{4}$			
f $\frac{3}{10}$			
g $\frac{4}{5}$			
h $\frac{1}{8}$			

4 Work out the sale prices.

a

$\frac{1}{3}$ off
£60

b

£15 $\frac{1}{2}$ price

I can find fractions of amounts.

12.4 More about percentages

1 Change these percentages into hundredths and decimals.

a 21% = ☐/☐ = _____

b 77% = ☐/☐ = _____

c 14% = ☐/☐ = _____

d 55% = ☐/☐ = _____

e 17% = ☐/☐ = _____

f 99% = ☐/☐ = _____

2 Change each test result into a percentage, using equivalent fractions.

a $\frac{32}{50}$ =

b $\frac{17}{50}$ =

c $\frac{47}{50}$ =

d $\frac{21}{25}$ =

e $\frac{8}{25}$ =

f $\frac{15}{25}$ =

g $\frac{14}{20}$ =

h $\frac{6}{20}$ =

i $\frac{19}{20}$ =

j Which test result is the highest? ☐ Which is the lowest? ☐

3 Inflation has increased the cost of these travel tickets. What are the new prices?

a 10% increase

b 20% increase

c 25% increase

ticket: £25

ticket: £60

ticket: £300

£25 + ☐ = ☐

£60 + ☐ = ☐

£300 + ☐ = ☐

4 Use a calculator to find the percentage of each amount.

a 75% of £120 = _____

b 56% of £90 = _____

c 49% of £150 = _____

d 17% of £45 = _____

e 99% of £500 = _____

f 9% of £30 = _____

5 How much do you save?

30% off   £250

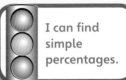

I can find simple percentages.

12.5 Ratio and proportion

1 Write the ratio of blue to red.

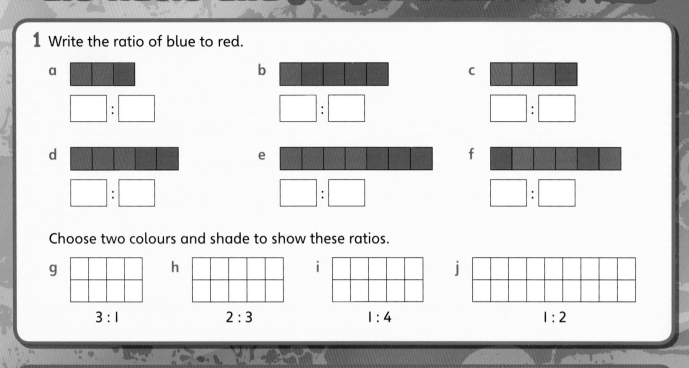

a   ⬜ : ⬜   b   ⬜ : ⬜   c   ⬜ : ⬜

d   ⬜ : ⬜   e   ⬜ : ⬜   f   ⬜ : ⬜

Choose two colours and shade to show these ratios.

g   h   i   j

   3 : 1   2 : 3   1 : 4   1 : 2

2 Dave needs these ingredients to make a cake for 4 people:

     300 g flour   180 g sugar   200 g butter

How much of each ingredient does Dave need to make cakes for:

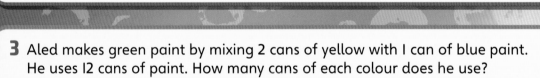

		flour	sugar	butter
a	8 people			
b	40 people			
c	6 people			

Remember!
A **ratio** is
1 for every ...

A **proportion** is
1 in every ...

3 Aled makes green paint by mixing 2 cans of yellow with 1 can of blue paint.
He uses 12 cans of paint. How many cans of each colour does he use?

Colour the cans to help you find how much of each is needed.

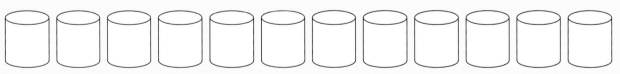

Yellow   Blue

4 In a class are 2 boys for every 3 girls.
There are 10 boys. How many girls are there?

I can answer
word problems
using ratio.

12.6 More about ratio

1 Solve these word problems using ratio.

Purple paint can be made from 3 parts red paint to 2 parts blue paint.

  a 300 ml of red paint is used.
     How much blue paint is needed?

  b 100 ml of blue paint is used.
     How much red paint is needed?

The metal bronze is made of a mix of 9 parts copper to 1 part tin.

  c 2 kg of tin is used.
     How much copper is needed?

  d 36 kg of copper is used.
     How much tin is used?

2 Jo decides to decorate her bathroom. She buys 1 box of white tiles and 4 boxes of patterned blue tiles. Design a blue tile, and then make up a pattern she could use.

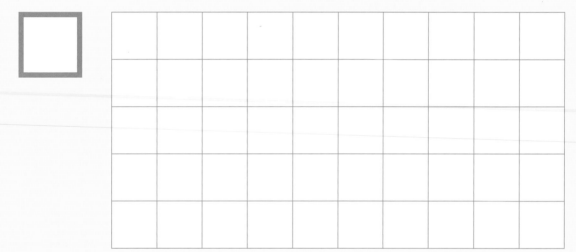

3 Ben has 24 books. He has 5 fiction books for every 3 non-fiction books.

How many fiction books does he have? How many non-fiction books does he have? Show your working.

> I like science fiction best!

Ben has _____ non-fiction books

and _____ fiction books.

4 The baker always makes two brown rolls to every three white rolls. Today he has made 30 bread rolls. How many brown rolls has he made? How many white rolls has he made?

Brown [ ]   White [ ]

I can divide a ratio into two parts.

13.1 Coordinates and functions

1 a Make (x, y) coordinates from these tables of values. Then plot each set of coordinates on the grid. Join up the points into two straight lines and label them $x = 4$ and $y = 3$.

$x = 4$

x	4	4	4	4	4
y	0	2	4	6	8

coordinates ($\underline{4}$,$\underline{0}$)(__,__)(__,__)(__,__)(__,__)

$y = 3$

x	0	2	4	6	8
y	3	3	3	3	3

coordinates (__,__)(__,__)(__,__)(__,__)(__,__)

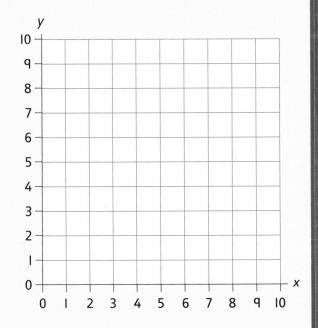

b Now draw the lines $x = 7$ and $y = 6$ on the grid and label them.

2 a Write the output numbers for these function machines.

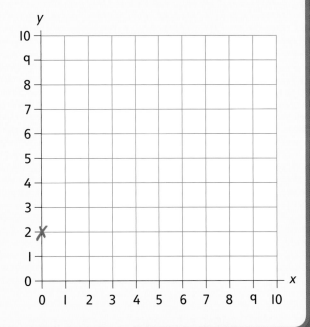

b Use the input and output numbers to make coordinate pairs. Plot the coordinates and join them into straight lines on the empty grid. Label the lines $y = 2x + 2$ and $y = 2x - 1$.

3 Write the coordinates of all the points where the lines cross in the graphs in question 1.

(__,__) (__,__) (__,__) (__,__)

I can read coordinates.

13.2 Real-life graphs

1 Recipe books often list the weights of ingredients in pounds and ounces (imperial) and kg and grams (metric).

Use the approximate conversion of I ounce (oz) = 30 grams (g) to fill in the missing measures.

a   I oz   __30__ g

b   2 oz   _____ g

c   _____ oz   I20 g

d   _____ oz   240 g

e   I2 oz   _____ g

2 a   Use the values in question I to plot points on the grid and make a conversion graph between metric and imperial measures of weight.

Conversion graph

(Graph: vertical axis "Metric (grams)" marked 0, 50, 100, 150, 200, 250, 300, 350, 400, 450, 500. Horizontal axis "Imperial (ounces)" marked 0, 2, 4, 6, 8, 10, 12, 14, 16. A point X is plotted near 1 oz, 30 g.)

Hint!
I pound (lb) = I6 ounces (oz)

I kg = I000 g

Use the conversion graph to find the approximate equivalent measures.

b   3 oz = _____ g

c   II oz = _____ g

d   I50 g = _____ oz

e   I75 g = _____ oz

f   200 g = _____ oz

g   I kg 200 g = _____ lb _____ oz

h   I lb I0 oz = _____ g

3 a   I6 oz (I lb) is approximately _____ grams.

b   I kg is approximately _____ lb _____ oz.

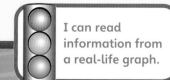

I can read information from a real-life graph.

13.3 Multiples and factors

1 a Write the missing multiples and complete this multiplication table.

x	2	3	4	5	6	7	8	9	10
2									
3									
4									
5	10								
6									
7								70	
8									
9									
10									

Use the multiplication table in part **a** to find **factor pairs** for these numbers.

> **Remember!**
> I is a factor of every number, and every number is a factor of itself.

b 10: __2, 5__

c 70: __7, 10__

d 15: _____

e 12: _____ and _____

f 20: _____ and _____

g 30: _____ and _____

h 24: _____ and _____

---

2 Use tests of divisibility, the table in question I and a calculator to find the factors of these numbers. Use the examples to help.

Examples

- **39** is divisible by I, 3 and 39; 39 ÷ 3 = 13, so 13 is also a factor of 39.

- **44** is divisible by I, 2, 4 and 44; 44 ÷ 2 = 22, 44 ÷ 4 = II, so II and 22 are also factors of 44.

a **28**   I, _____, _____, _____, _____, 28

b **36**   I, _____, _____, _____, _____, _____, _____, _____ 36

c **45**   _____, _____, _____, _____, _____, _____

d **66**   _____, _____, _____, _____. _____, _____, _____, _____

3

> 81   3   24   20   5   8

Using each number only once, choose a number from the coloured oval which is:

a a multiple of 5 _____

b a factor of I0 _____

c a multiple of 6 _____

d a factor of 6 _____

e divisible by 9 _____

f a factor of 32 _____

---

4 Find four factors of:

a **40**   _____, _____, _____, _____

b **42**   _____, _____, _____, _____

> I can find factors of 2-digit numbers.

13.4 Prime numbers

1 List the numbers between 2 and 30 that do **not** appear in the multiplication table in 13.3.

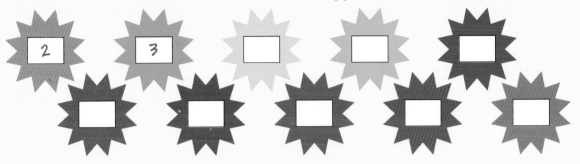

2   3

What is the special name of these numbers? _____

2 Look at the numbers below. Use tests of divisibility or a calculator to see if they have any factors other than themselves and 1. Write each number in the correct shape.

31   33   35   37   39   41   43   45   47   49   51   53   55   57   59

prime numbers

not prime numbers

3 Draw a line to join each number to the correct label.

> **Remember!**
> 1 is not a prime number.

a factor of 8   **b** prime number   **c** multiple of 8

16   11   2   24   19   7   4   8

4 Ring the prime numbers in this list:

9   29   49   69   89   99

I can check whether a number is prime.

13.5 Common multiples and factors

1 Write the multiples of the bottom number in the ladders.

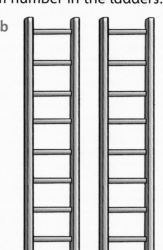

a

(18)

12

6

27

(18)

9

b

8

12

c

15

20

d Ring the numbers that are the same in each pair. These are **common multiples**.

Fill in the table.

Numbers	Common multiples
6 and 9	18
8 and 12	
15 and 20	

2 Write the factors of each number. Then ring the numbers that appear in both lists. These are **common factors**.

a **18**   1, __2__, __3__, _____, _____, _____,

    24   1, __2__, _____, _____, _____, _____, _____, 24

b **32**   1, _____, _____, _____, _____, 32

    48   1, _____, _____, _____, _____, _____, _____, _____, _____, 48

3 Write three numbers that are:

a prime   _____, _____, _____

b factors of 36   _____, _____, _____

c multiples of 22   _____, _____, _____

I understand the difference between prime numbers, factors and multiples.

1 In each sequence the steps are the same size. Write the missing numbers and the rule.

a 15 ☐ ☐ ☐ 59   Rule: _____

b 94 ☐ ☐ ☐ ☐ 54   Rule: _____

c 1.5 ☐ ☐ 5.7   Rule: _____

2 Draw a line to connect each sequence to its rule.

a 25, 125, 625, 3125

b 60, 6, 0.6, 0.06

c 2, 7, 17, 37

d 98, 48, 23, 10.5

e 600, 120, 24, 4.8

×2 +3

−2 ÷2

×5

÷5

÷10

3 Work out the mystery numbers.

a It is a multiple of 3 and a factor of 12. It is not prime.   ☐

b It is a prime number between 10 and 20. It is a factor of 77.   ☐

c Half of this number is a prime and a factor of 20.   ☐

d It is a multiple of 3 and of 5. It is a factor of 45.   ☐

e Use different factors of 48 in each box:

☐ × ☐ = 48   and   ☐ × ☐ = 48

48 ÷ ☐ = ☐   and   48 ÷ ☐ = ☐

f The mystery number is 20. Write a question for it using **factor** and **multiple**.

4 My mystery number is between 15 and 55. It is a factor of 100 and a multiple of 5. What could it be?

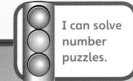

I can solve number puzzles.

13.7 Sequences and rules

1 Write the first five terms of each sequence.

a First term 5, add 6. _____

b First term 100, subtract 5. _____

c First term 2, add 1 then multiply by 3. _____

d First term 102, subtract 2 then divide by 2. _____

2 Draw the next two patterns in each sequence. Then fill in the table showing how many shapes are in each pattern. Work out the rule and the next three terms without drawing them.

a

Shape number	1	2	3	4	5	6	7	8
Number of circles	1	5						

Rule: _____

b

Shape number	1	2	3	4	5	6	7	8
Number of sticks	6							

Rule: _____

3 a If the first Saturday in January is the 3rd, write the dates of all the Saturdays in January.

_____

b Write the sequence of the first day of each month for the year.

_____

4 Write the first five terms of this sequence: start at 50, subtract 11.

I can generate a sequence from a rule.

13.8 Substituting and using formulae

1 Write each expression as simply as possible.

a $a + a + a + b + b =$ _____

b $x + y + z + x + y =$ _____

c $2p + 3q + p + 2q =$ _____

d $5r + 4s - 2r - s =$ _____

Write the perimeter of each shape in terms of x.

e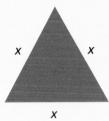

f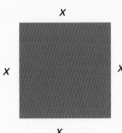

g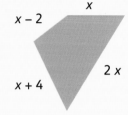

h Work out the perimeter of each shape in parts **e**, **f** and **g** when $x = 4$ cm.

---

2 Use the formula **£1 = $2** to convert pounds into dollars and dollars into pounds.

a £3 = $_____

b £8 = $_____

c $10 = £_____

d $30 = £_____

e £2.50 = $_____

f $9 = £_____

g £3.25 = $_____

h $12.50 = £_____

Bobbie is 5 years older than Andy. Use the formula **A = B − 5** to work out their ages.

i Work out Andy's age when Bobbie is: 10 _____   21 _____   43 _____

j Work out Bobbie's age when Andy is: 14 _____   27 _____   49 _____

---

3 Some friends are planning a picnic. Each person will need:

4 sandwiches   2 pieces of fruit $\frac{1}{2}$ litre juice

a If **p** is the number of people going on the picnic, write a formula for each item.

sandwiches: **s = 4p**   fruit: _____   juice: _____

> **Remember!**
> Choose a letter to represent each item, e.g. **s** for sandwiches.

b Use the formulae to work out how much of each item they need for:

• 6 people _____

• 9 people _____

---

4 A mobile phone call abroad costs 25p per minute, plus 10p connection charge. How much does a 10 minute call cost?

> I can substitute into a simple formula given in words.

14.1 Space solver

1 A holiday cottage has a living room, a bedroom, a toilet, a bathroom and a small kitchen. On opening the front door you walk into an octagonal hallway.

    a On a sheet of centimetre squared paper, draw a horizontal axis from 0 to 22 and a vertical axis from 0 to 12. The scale of the plan is 1 cm : 1 m.

    b Plot these coordinate points:

        (1,1)   (22,1)   (22,11)   (1,11)

        Join the points to make the outside walls of the cottage.

    c Plot and join these points to make the octagonal hall:

        (12,1)   (10,3)   (10,5)   (12,7)   (14,7)   (16,5)   (16,3)   (14,1)

    d On your grid, design your own plan of the cottage, showing the five rooms. Make sure the sizes of your rooms are appropriate.

> **Hint!**
> Test them by pacing:
> 1 large pace is approximately 1 metre.

    e What shapes are the rooms?

        kitchen   _____   living room _____

        bedroom _____   bathroom _____

        toilet   _____

    f What are the coordinates of the bedroom? _____

    g Measure three different angles on your plan. Label them A, B and C.

        A = _____°   B = _____°   C = _____°

    h What is the rule for finding the area of a rectangle? _____

    i What is the floor area of the whole cottage?

2 Peggy wants to put a ribbon border around the edges of a square cushion. The sides of the cushion are 40 cm. She has 1.5 m of ribbon. Does she have enough ribbon to complete the border? Show all your thinking and working.

> I can solve a problem involving shape, space and measures.

14.2 Number problems

1 When the library shelf is full there are 125 books. At the moment there are only 86 books on the shelf. How many books are on loan?

2 My sister is half my age and my mother is 5 times older than my sister. I am 12 years old. My father is 7 years older than my mother.

   a How old is my sister?

   b How old is my mother?

   c How old is my father?

3 Official statistics show that in 2002:

- 166 children were killed on the roads
- 96 children drowned
- 917 498 were injured in falls and taken to hospital.

How many children is this altogether?

4 What is the total cost of one ruler, one eraser and one pencil?

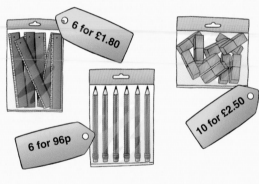

6 for £1.80

10 for £2.50

6 for 96p

5 A shed measures 4.3 m by 2.75 m. Sam needs to replace the gutter all around the shed. How much guttering should he buy?

6 a What is the total cost of buying a DVD for £7.49 and a CD costing £11.99?

   b What is the change from a £20 note?

I can solve a problem involving money.

14.3 Data problems

1 The picture shows the tip of a giant's thumb, from his first knuckle to the tip.

Problem **How tall is this giant likely to be?**

To solve the problem, work through the steps below.

a Collect this information from 10 volunteers and record it in the table.

Thumb tip length										
Height										

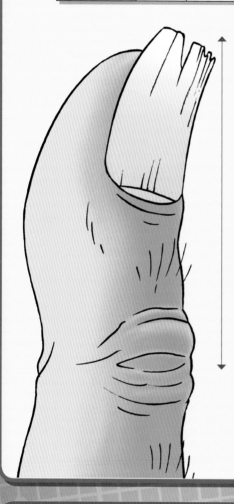

b Decide whether to use the **median** or the **mode** of this data and explain why.

_____

_____

c The median/mode length of the thumb tip in your data sample is _____

d The median/mode height in your data sample is _____

e The length of the giant's thumb tip is _____

f How many times greater is the giant's thumb tip than the average from your data sample? _____

g Work out the likely height of the giant. _____

2 The data shows how many photos some pupils in Leo's class took on their mobile phones last week.

    22   13   62   11   22   14   13   11   16   22   45

a The most popular number of photos taken is _____

This is called the _____

b The median number of photos taken is _____

I can solve a problem using data.

1 Work out the missing prices in this Continental breakfast menu.

Menu

Croissant	45p
Croissant and yoghurt	£1.00
Croissant, yoghurt and hot chocolate	£1.85
Hot chocolate and croissant	_____
Yoghurt and hot chocolate	_____

2 The perimeter of a tablecloth is 300 cm. The cloth is twice as long as it is wide.

Find the width and the length of the tablecloth.

Hint! Use trial and improvement.

3 Pupils will have a detention if they do not have at least three of the following items of equipment:

ruler   eraser   pencil

pen   sharpener

a   List all the possible combinations of three items they could have. Make up a sensible coding system.

b   Now list the possible ways of having four items and five items.

4 Show your working in the table below.

- Choose a number, add 3, double the answer, subtract 6 and then halve it. What number have you ended up with?

- Try this again, starting with a different number. What happens?

- Try it again, using the letter *m* to stand for a million or any other number.

Choose a number			m
Add 3			
Double			
Subtract 6			
Halve			

5 Some farmers and some sheep are in a barn. Altogether, there are 12 heads and 42 legs! How many sheep and how many farmers are there?

I can solve a problem by trying different numbers.

14.5 Ratio problems

1 A small bottle of lemonade costs £1.20. A larger bottle costs one and a half times as much.

   a   How much does the larger bottle cost? _____

   b   Do you think that the larger bottle will hold one and a half times as much?

       Explain your thinking. _____

2

   Around three-quarters of all the journeys made in the UK are short enough to be made using a bicycle.

   Brenda decides she will use her bicycle for $\frac{3}{4}$ of her daily journeys. She estimates that she makes about 20 short journeys per week.

   a   How many journeys will she now make on her bicycle?

       _____

   b   Give two reasons why this is good thing.

3 In a survey, 60 pupils were asked which school subject they enjoyed the most:

   • 40% liked PE best

   • $\frac{1}{3}$ liked mathematics

   • $\frac{1}{12}$ enjoyed ICT

   • the rest voted for art

   How many pupils like art best?

4 50 people chose an instrument at a musical carnival.

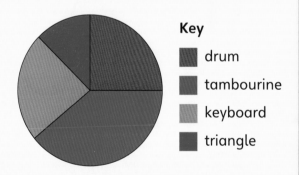

Key

   ▨ drum
   ▨ tambourine
   ▨ keyboard
   ▨ triangle

   a   Estimate the fraction of people who chose a drum.

       _____

   b   Estimate how many people chose a tambourine.

       _____

   c   Estimate the ratio of those who chose a drum to those who chose a triangle.

       _____

5 Abel's tomato soup recipe needs 6 tomatoes for every $\frac{1}{2}$ litre of water. He uses 24 tomatoes. How much water does he need?

I can solve problems involving ratio.

14.6 Puzzles

1 You have three 1s, three 2s and three 3s.

Write the numbers on the grid so that each row and each column adds up to 6.

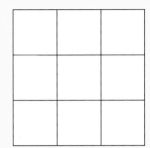

> **Hint!**
> Write the numbers on pieces of paper to try out some ideas.

3 Write the numbers 7, 8, 9, 20, 21 and 22 in the circles so that each side of the triangle adds up to the same number.

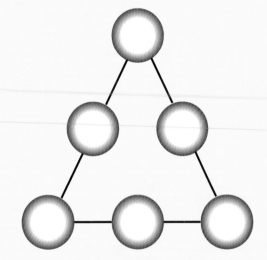

2 Work out the value of each symbol.

Then work out what the missing totals are.

ⓘ = _____   📞 = _____

🌧 = _____   ✈ = _____

ⓘ	ⓘ	ⓘ	ⓘ	12
✈	ⓘ	✈	✈	9
🌧	✈	ⓘ	📞	[ ]
🌧	🌧	📞	📞	30

15   [ ]   18   [ ]

4 Explain why an **odd** number + an **odd** number *always* makes an **even** number.

Use a diagram to help you.

5 Four children have 37 merits between them.

- Phil has 5 fewer than Khalid.
- Jane has twice as many as Khalid.
- Aled has 2 more than Khalid.

How many merits does each child have?

Khalid _____

Phil _____

Jane _____

Aled _____

> **Hint!**
> Try a number for Khalid first, and use the table to work out the other children's numbers.

Khalid	Phil	Jane	Aled	*Total*

I can solve a problem by thinking mathematically.

15.1 3-D shapes

1 Write the name of each 3-D shape below the picture.

a

_____

b

_____

c

_____

d

_____

e

_____

f

_____

g

_____

h

_____

i

_____

2 What am I?

a   I am half a sphere. What am I?   _____

b   I have 2 circular faces. What am I?   _____

c   I have 5 faces. 4 faces are triangular. What am I?   _____

d   I am a prism. I have 2 triangular faces. What am I?   _____

e   I have 6 faces, but not all are square. What am I?   _____

f   I have 6 vertices, and my faces are triangular. What am I? _____

3 Use the words **faces**, **edges** and **vertices** to describe:

a   a cube

b   a tetrahedron

I can identify faces, edges and vertices on 3-D shapes.

15.2 Nets

1 a Ring the shapes that are nets of an **open cube**.

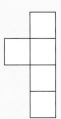 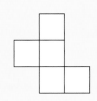

b Only one of these is a net of a **closed cube**. Tick it.

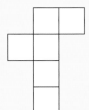 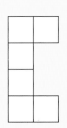 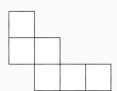

2 Which shapes are not nets of a cuboid? Why?

A 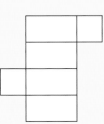   B 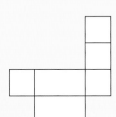   C 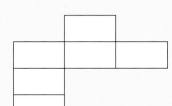   D

3 Which one of these designs is the net of a closed cube?

A 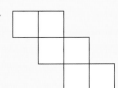   B

I can identify nets of a closed cube.

15.3 More nets

1 a Draw triangles to make different nets of a tetrahedron.

b Draw shapes to make different nets of a square-based pyramid.

2 Which of these is not the net of a triangular prism? Why?

A   B   C

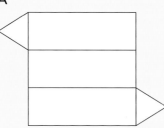 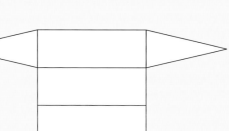 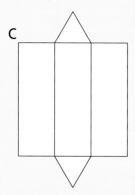

3 Draw the net of an octahedron.

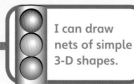
I can draw
nets of simple
3-D shapes.

15.4 2-D pictures of 3-D shapes

1 a This is one face of a 3-D shape. Which 3-D shapes could it be?

_____

b If every face is like this, what shape could it be? _____

c If another face was a square, what shape could it be? _____

2 Make a shape with 8 interlocking cubes.

Draw what you can see from the front, the right-hand side and the top (plan view).

front	side	plan

3 Look carefully at this shape.

Try to visualise its front and side views and its plan. Draw them.

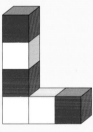

front	right-hand side	plan

I can visualise
3-D shapes from
2-D drawings.

15.5 Drawing 3-D shapes

1 Draw the missing edges and finish these 3-D shapes.

What shapes did you make?

a _____

b _____

c _____

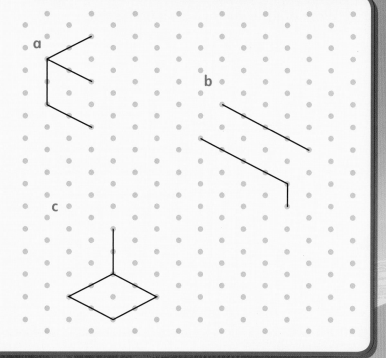

2 Draw a cube and cuboid in the space below.

Use a ruler and a set square to help draw the shapes accurately.

3 Now sketch these 3-D shapes.

   a squared-based pyramid   **b** tetrahedron

   c triangular prism   **d** octahedron

Use the actual shapes to help you.

I can sketch 3-D shapes.

15.6 Surface area

1 Work out the **surface area** of this cube.

Show your working.

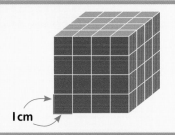

1 cm

2 a Each face on this cube has an area of 100 cm². How long and wide are the sides?

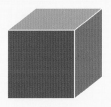

b What is the surface area of the cube?

3 a Draw the net of a cuboid. Four faces should measure 3 cm × 2 cm.

b What is the area of one 3 cm × 2 cm face?

c What is the area of the whole net? Show your working.

4 What is the area of this rectangle?

5 cm

3 cm

I can work out the area of a rectangle by multiplying its length by its width.

15.7 Volume

1 What is the **volume** of this cube?

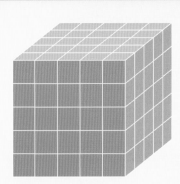

Hint!
How many cubes
are in a layer?
How many layers
are there?

Volume = _____ cubes

2 Make a cuboid from 20 interlocking cubes.

a   Sketch it here.

b   What is its surface area?

c   What is its volume?

3 Make another shape using 20 interlocking cubes. It can be any shape you like.

a   Sketch the shape.

b   What is the volume of the shape?

4 What is the volume of this shape?

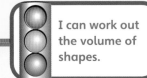

I can work out
the volume of
shapes.

15.8 Compass points

1 Draw a diagram to show these compass points: N, S, E, W, NW, NE, SW and SE.

2 Collect the triangles! Write a route from one triangle to another. Begin with the red triangle.

Write the coordinates of each triangle and the direction of travel.

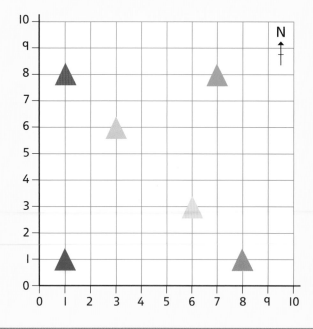

3 a Draw the route from Junction 9 to the car park **P** beside the High Street following these directions: NE, E, SE, SW.

b Now make up your own route from the car park **P** to the railway station .

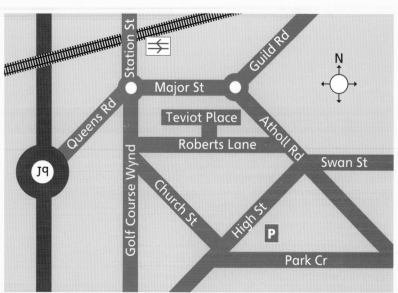

15.9 Problem solving

1 Sam Smiths' crisp factory want a new logo for their product. They want the logo to be a quadrilateral with the letters **SS** in the middle.

Draw three types of quadrilateral in the grid and list their names and the coordinates for the corners of each.

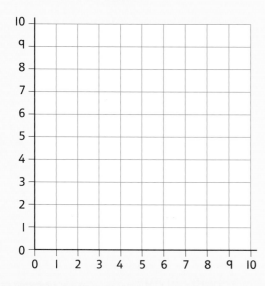

Name of quadrilateral _____

Coordinates _____

Name of quadrilateral _____

Coordinates _____

Name of quadrilateral _____

Coordinates _____

2 Charlie Choc & Co. want new packaging for their chocolates. They do not want to use cube and cuboid shapes. Sketch a 3-D shape that they could use, draw its net, and write its name.

3 a Kathy needs to know how much space boxes like the one below will take up in her office. She has ten boxes. Work out how much space they will take up.

Volume of I box: _____ cubes

Volume of I0 boxes: _____ cubes

b Kathy wants to vacuum pack each box. She needs to find out the surface area of each box. What is it?

Surface area of I box: _____ square units

I can solve a problem involving shape and measures.

16.1 Frequency tables

1 Robert interviewed 28 people about how many coins they had in their pockets.

He has put some of the results in a table.

a Fill the gaps in the table.

Number of coins	Tally	Frequency
0–3		5
4–7	𝍇 II	
8–11	III	
12–15		
16–19		3
20 or more	𝍇 I	

b What was the most common answer?

_____

c How many people had more than 11 coins in their pocket?

_____

2 Two teams competed in the National Tiddlywinks Grand Final. The scores of the six matches are shown in the table.

Westwood Winners	14	19	7	22	12	13
Caludon Champions	17	18	13	20	10	24

a Who won more matches?

_____

b What was the total score for:

- Westwood Winners _____
- Caludon Champions _____

c What was the biggest winning margin? _____

d Who would you crown National Champion?

_____

3 A head teacher collected attendance data for Years 7, 8 and 9. She produced a table for each of two Year groups and a bar chart for the other Year group but didn't label them properly.

Use the information in the statements to label the tables and the bar chart with the correct Year group.

- In Year 7 more people have 3 lates than 2 lates.
- In Year 8 the number of 1 late is double the number of 4 lates.
- In Year 9 the same number of people have 2, 3 and 5 lates.

Year _____

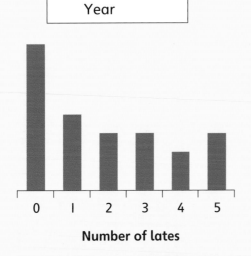

Number of lates

Year _____

Lates	Frequency
0	6
1	4
2	4
3	3
4	2
5	1

Year _____

Lates	Frequency
0	8
1	6
2	2
3	4
4	2
5	1

I can find information from frequency tables and bar charts.

16.2 Bar charts

1 The frequency table shows the recent test scores for 9M3. The data has been **grouped**.

Result	Frequency
0–10	2
11–20	3
21–30	8
31–40	9
41–50	6

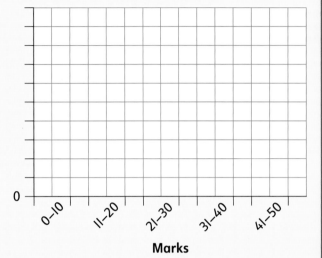

Marks

a Use the information to draw a bar chart.

b How many pupils took the test? _____

c The pass mark was 31 marks.
How many pupils passed? _____

2 This table shows how many copies of two computer games a shop sold each day for a week.

	Mon	Tue	Wed	Thur	Fri	Sat	Sun
Super Marco 3	20	5	30	15	35	70	55
Tonic the Warthog	25	20	25	15	45	65	60

a Draw a dual bar chart to show number of games sold each day.

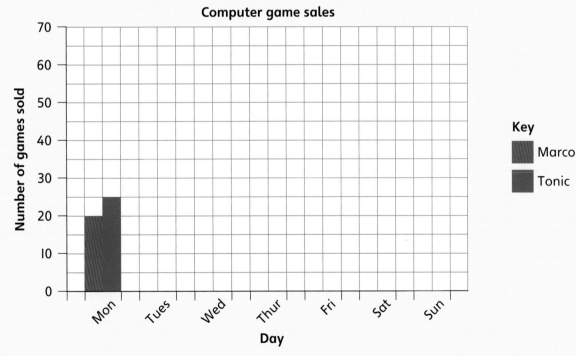

Key
Marco
Tonic

b How many games in total were sold on Friday? _____

c On which day did they sell the fewest games? _____

d Why did the shop sell more games on Saturday and Sunday?

_____

I can draw a dual bar chart.

16.3 Questionnaires and surveys

A pizza company wants to build a new restaurant in your area. They have asked you to help do some market research to make sure the restaurant meets the needs of its customers.

1 The pizza company wants to know how much customers will spend on a large pizza.

   a Write a question they can ask.

   _____

   b Ask your classmates your question. Record your results in the frequency table.

Amount	Tally	Frequency
£0–£2.99		
£3–£5.99		
£6–£8.99		
£9 or more		

2 The pizza company also wants to know how often people eat pizza. This will help them decide whether to offer a takeaway service.

   a Write a question they can ask.

   _____

   b Fill in four options for people to choose from. Carry out a survey and record the results.

Number of times	Tally	Frequency

Don't forget to include a time period.

3 The pizza company wants to know what the most popular toppings are.

Write a question, carry out a survey with four choices of toppings, and record your results in the frequency table.

Question: _____

Pizza topping	Tally	Frequency
1		
2		
3		
4		

I can design a question to collect data.

You have been asked to report your findings from your survey to the management of the pizza company. You need to be accurate and present your findings professionally.

1 Use your information to draw a bar chart to show how much customers will spend on a large pizza.

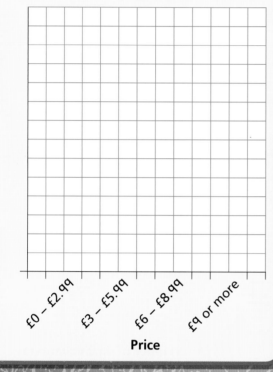

Frequency

£0 – £2.99   £3 – £5.99   £6 – £8.99   £9 or more

Price

2 Use your information to draw a bar chart to show how often customers eat pizza.

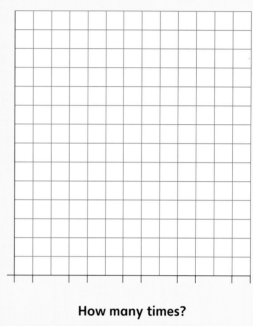

Frequency

How many times?

3 Draw a bar chart to show the most popular pizza toppings.

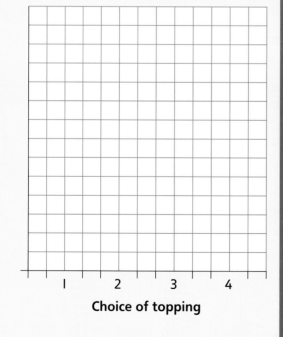

Frequency

1   2   3   4

Choice of topping

4 Using your reports, the pizza company has predicted how much profit it will make over the next 6 months.

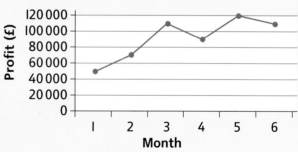

Profit (£)

120 000
100 000
80 000
60 000
40 000
20 000
0

1   2   3   4   5   6

Month

a In which month do they think they will make the most profit?

_____

b How much money do they plan to make in the first six months altogether?

_____

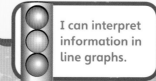

I can interpret information in line graphs.

16.5 Mode, median and range

1 The bar chart shows the number of holidays taken in the past two years by a group of families.

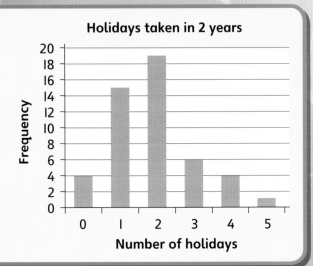

Holidays taken in 2 years

a What is the range of the number of holidays?

_____

b What is the modal number of holidays?

_____

c How many families took part in the survey?

_____

2 400 website visitors were asked how many mp3 files they had downloaded over the past month. This grouped bar chart shows the results.

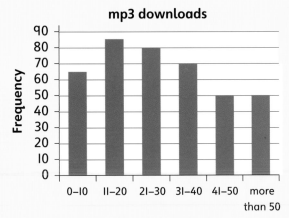

mp3 downloads

a How many people downloaded 0–10 mp3 files?

_____

b How many people downloaded more than 50 mp3 files?

_____

c What is the modal class?

_____

3 Find the mode and range of each set of data.

a 7, 4, 3, 8, 3, 9, 6, 7, 8, 7, 9   Mode _____   Range _____

b 25.5, 29, 18.5, 22.5, 23, 25.5, 24   Mode _____   Range _____

4 Find the median value of each set of data. Write the numbers in order first.

a 12, 3, 8, 9, 7, 5, 2, 9, 6   _____   Median _____

b 8, 5, 8, 3, 4, 5, 6, 9   _____   Median _____

5 Ayla recorded the time her classmates took to run around the school playground. The times are measured in seconds: 42, 38, 49, 52, 42, 42, 38, 32, 34, 38, 32, 42, 36

Find the mode, range and median for the data.

a Mode _____   b Range _____   c Median _____

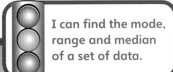

I can find the mode, range and median of a set of data.

16.6 Comparing distributions

1 Tahmid and Lauren are competing for a place in the Striking Arrows darts team.
These are their scores with 10 sets of darts.

Tahmid	130	160	100	120	160	115	120	171	110	120
Lauren	60	157	150	70	155	170	150	90	80	150

   a Find the range for both players.

      Tahmid: _____   Lauren: _____

   b Find the mode for both players.

      Tahmid: _____   Lauren: _____

   c Which player should the Striking Arrows select for the team?   _____

      Why? _____

2 A teacher measured the height of classes in different year groups. Some of the results are in the table.

   a Work out and fill in the missing values.

   b Which year group has the biggest range? Why do you think this might be?

	Range	Shortest	Tallest
Year 7	22 cm	132 cm	
Year 9		130 cm	167 cm
Year 11	27 cm		172 cm

     _____

3 Some boys and girls were asked how many video games they had bought in the last month. The information is represented in two bar charts.

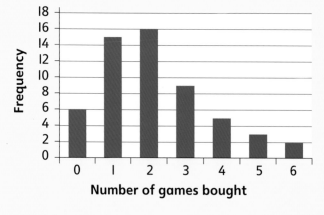

Number of games bought by boys

Number of games bought by girls

   a Which group has the bigger range? _____

   b What is the mode for: girls _____   boys _____

   c How many games did the girls buy in total?

     _____

> I can use mode and range to compare two sets of data.

16.7 Fairground games

1 The first game uses two spinners as shown here.

To win a prize both spinners must show the same colour.

A B

certain	likely	even chance
unlikely	impossible	

Use the words in the box to complete the sentences.

a Getting red on spinner A is

_____

b Getting blue on spinner B is

_____

c Getting yellow on spinner A is

_____

d Getting blue or red on spinner B is

_____

e Getting white on spinner B is

_____

2 The second game involves rolling a 10-sided dice.

- To win a big prize you need to roll a multiple of 5.

- To win a small prize you need to roll a multiple of 3.

The bar chart shows how many times each number was rolled during one day.

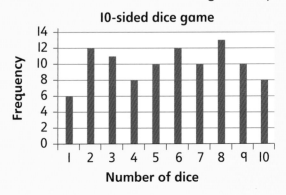

a How many big prizes were won? _____

b How many small prizes were won?

_____

c Use the bar chart and work out the probability of not winning a prize.

_____

3 In the final game you choose a duck at random from a set of 12 ducks.

Each duck has a shape on the bottom:

4 ducks have a star   3 ducks have a square

I duck has a triangle   the rest have circles

a How many ducks have circles? _____

b Do this experiment.

Shape	Tally	Frequency
Star		
Square		
Triangle		
Circle		

- Get 12 small pieces of paper.

- On each piece, draw a shape to match the shapes on the ducks.

- Put the pieces of paper in a bag or a box.

- Draw a piece of paper at random 30 times.

- Record the results in the table.

c Which shape was most common in your experiment? _____

d From your experiment, what is the probability of choosing a square? _____

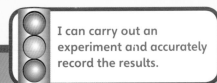

I can carry out an experiment and accurately record the results.

Revision

Quick quiz

1 Fill the gaps in this table.

Percentage	Fraction	Decimal
a	$\frac{1}{10}$	
b 40%		
c		0.85

→ *See 12.2*

2 Complete this function machine.

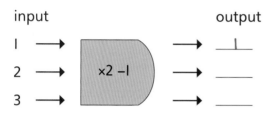

input   output

1 ⟶   ⟶ ___
2 ⟶   ×2 −1   ⟶ ___
3 ⟶   ⟶ ___

→ *See 13.1*

3 The bar chart shows how many days the pupils in a class were absent during the previous fortnight.

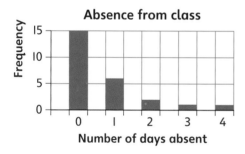

How many pupils are in the class?

_____

→ *See 16.2*

4 List the factors of 20.

_____

→ *See 13.3*

5 Which rectangle has greater area: one that is 8 cm × 7 cm or another 6 cm × 9 cm?

→ *See 15.6*

6

a What is the name of this shape?

_____

b How many faces does it have? _____

c How many edges does it have? _____

→ *See 15.1*

7 In a shoe shop the ratio of shoes to boots is 3:1. Pick numbers from the box to complete these sentences correctly.

$\frac{1}{3}$ $\frac{1}{4}$ 3   4

a There are _____ times as many shoes as boots.

b The number of boots is _____ the total number of boots and shoes.

→ *See 12.5, 14.5*

8 Amy's mother gave her £2 and asked her to buy two tins of baked beans at 32p each, a packet of margarine costing 59p and a loaf of bread at 54p. Amy could keep the change. How much change could Amy keep?

→ *See 14.2*

9 The formula for the area of a triangle is:

area = (base × height) ÷ 2

Use this to find the area of a triangle that has a base of 8 cm and a height of 5 cm.

→ *See 13.8*

10 a What is 10% of £65? _____

b What is the price of a £65 suit if it is sold at 10% off?

_____

→ *See 12.4,*

Revision

Check up questions

1 Tommy has *n* items in his pencil case.

Jayne has 2 more items than Tommy. Philip has 4 fewer items than Tommy. Dahl has 2 more than Jayne, and Briony has twice as many items as Tommy.

Match the names and the labels.

Briony   Dahl   Tommy   Philip

n $n-4$ $2n$ $n+4$

→ See 13.8

2

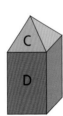

a Name the 4 solids used in these towers.

A: _____

B: _____

C: _____

D: _____

b Draw the net of a cube.

→ See 15.1, 15.2

3 Last week a pensioner spent $\frac{4}{7}$ of his £98 pension on food, 20% on heating and 15% on other bills. Use a calculator to work out how much money he spent on:

a food   _____

b heating   _____

c other bills   _____

→ See 12.3, 12.4, 14.2

4 a Calculate $\frac{3}{5}$ of 60 metres.

b Calculate 55% of £60.

c Which is larger: $\frac{3}{5}$ or 55%? _____

→ See 12.2–12.4

5 Sue rolled a dice 20 times. Here are her results:

3 3 4 2 5 1 5 6 5 2
5 6 4 5 6 1 5 4 1 5

a Complete the frequency table.

Roll	Tally	Frequency
1		
2		
3		
4		
5		
6		

b What score is the mode? _____

c Do you think this is a fair or a biased dice? Give a reason for your answer.

_____

→ See 16.1, 16.5

6 a Write down a multiple of 6. _____

b Write down a factor of 16. _____

c Write down a prime number bigger than 10. _____

d Write down a number that is a factor of 21 and a prime number. _____

→ See 13.3, 13.4